Global Perspectives in Children's Literature

Evelyn B. Freeman

The Ohio State University

Barbara A. Lehman

The Ohio State University at Mansfield

Allyn and Bacon

Boston ▪ London ▪ Toronto ▪ Sydney ▪ Tokyo ▪ Singapore

Vice President: *Paul A. Smith*
Senior Editor: *Arnis E. Burvikovs*
Editorial Assistant: *Patrice Mailloux*
Marketing Manager: *Kathleen Morgan*
Editorial Production Service: *Chestnut Hill Enterprises, Inc.*
Manufacturing Buyer: *Julie McNeill*
Cover Administrator: *Kristina Mose-Libon*
Electronic Composition: *Omegatype Typography, Inc.*

Internet: www.abacon.com

Between the time Website information is gathered and published, some sites may have closed. Also, the transcription of URLs can result in typographical errors. The publisher would appreciate notification where these occur so that they may be corrected in subsequent editions.

Library of Congress Cataloging-in-Publication Data

Freeman, Evelyn B. (Evelyn Blossom)
    Global perspectives in children's literature / Evelyn B. Freeman, Barbara A. Lehman.
        p. cm.
    Includes bibliographical references and indexes.
    ISBN 0-205-30862-7
      1. Children's literature—History and criticism.   I. Lehman, Barbara A.   II. Title.

    PN1009.A1 F69 2000
    809'.89282—dc21

                                                                                    00-062066

Printed in the United States of America
10 9 8 7 6 5 4 3 2 1   RRD-VA   05 04 03 02 01 00

*To Rachel and Naomi, who experienced
the joys of studying and living abroad*

EBF

*To my parents, who gave me my first international
experiences and taught me to think globally*

BAL

CONTENTS

PREFACE

Prague, the Czech Republic, was our destination in the summer of 1996 when we presented a session on global perspectives in children's literature at the World Congress of the International Reading Association. The positive response to our presentation from educators around the world was the first step in encouraging us to think about writing this book. Then, in the fall of 1997, we participated in the regional conference sponsored by the International Board on Books for Young People in Albuquerque, New Mexico. As we discussed and interacted with colleagues, we came to realize the paucity of professional material in the area of international children's literature. Although reference sources with annotated bibliographies were available, very few books existed that discussed the history, theory and research, and classroom applications of international children's literature. Our book, which provides a description, rationale, critical examination, and classroom uses of global children's books, is intended to begin to fill this void.

Children in the United States have been reading international children's books for more than a century. Many children's literature classics are books translated from other countries—such as the stories of Hans Christian Andersen, the Grimm Brothers, Perrault, and Aesop. Interest in international children's literature has increased in recent years. Through international literature, children's horizons are expanded as they engage in reading a story not only set in another country but also written from an insider's perspective. Young readers are exposed to multiple ways of knowing about experiences and events. Universal themes can be explored in culturally specific ways, therefore enabling children to recognize and appreciate similarities and differences among their counterparts around the world.

The audience for this book—children's literature professors, preservice and inservice teachers, and librarians—shares a commitment to the value of literature for children. As we enter the twenty-first century, our world is shrinking due to global communications and increased mobility. Yet, at the same time, ethnic and cultural divides seem to be widening. Children's literature about other cultures around the world is a way to bring people together, to travel the globe, to bridge our differences, and to rejoice in our common joys and triumphs.

We hope this book helps you begin your journey of sharing international books with children. In the first chapter, we provide an introduction to the field by reviewing the status of children's literature around the world, as well as describing the historical context of international children's literature. We also set forth the definition of international children's literature used in this book. Chapter 2 discusses the value and importance of global children's literature by elaborating the benefits to both children and the curriculum. Specific links to multicultural education and Holocaust education will be described. In Chapter 3, we highlight issues in the field such as the availability of global children's literature and the complex issues of authenticity and translation. In addition, we explain how international books come to be published and distributed in the United States and provide suggestions on selecting and evaluating global children's literature. Chapter 4 focuses on contemporary trends in global children's literature and is organized by genre: picture books, fiction, informational books, biography/autobiography, folklore, and poetry. The last chapter presents ideas for sharing international books with children across the curriculum. This chapter includes five parts: theme studies, the beauty and power of language, content connections, genre study, and visual literacy. Throughout the book, you will find short biographical profiles of important figures in international children's literature, that is, authors, illustrators, and professional pioneers.

We want to acknowledge and thank many individuals who assisted us with this book. We are grateful to Mary Lou White and our professional colleagues in USBBY (United States Board on Books for Young People) who stimulated and encouraged our interest in international children's literature. Our graduate students and the teachers with whom we work responded to our ideas and shared their ideas about many of the children's books we discuss. We gained additional insights from our colleagues on the International Reading Association's Notable Books for a Global Society Committee, with whom we have reviewed many books since 1995. Sally Oddi, owner of Cover-to-Cover children's bookstore in Columbus, Ohio, generously gave her time and expertise to us. Patricia Scharer, our colleague at Ohio State with whom we will co-edit *Bookbird,* provided encouragement and support throughout the process. We are grateful to Kam Chi Chan, doctoral student at The Ohio State University, who assisted with various tasks related to this book. Our editor at Allyn and Bacon, Arnie Burvikovs, gave us guidance and encouragement, and the following reviewers offered valuable feedback and suggestions for the manuscript: Cyndi Giorgis—University of Nevada, Las Vegas; Judith Schoenfeld, Fallon Memorial School; and Lorraine Gerstl, Santa Catalina Lower School. Finally, we want to thank our spouses, Harvey Freeman and Dan Lehman, for their endless patience, advice, and support as we worked on this book.

CHAPTER

1 Introduction

For fifty-seven years my great-aunt Arizona hugged her students. She hugged them when their work was good, and she hugged them when it was not. She taught them . . . about the faraway places they would visit someday. "Have you been there?" the students asked. "Only in my mind," she answered. "But someday you will go." (Houston, 1992)

For great-aunt Arizona's students in a one-room school, surely one of the ways they learned about the faraway places they would visit was through literature that brought the world to their small village in the Blue Ridge Mountains of Appalachia in the United States. Like Arizona, with the riches of children's books, they could visit the far reaches of the globe in their minds, and their world was not restricted to tiny Henson Creek. We have the same opportunity to be "world travelers" today with international children's literature.

The world of children's literature is at once as universal and as unique as are the world's children. Mother Goose, for example, apparently has flown around the globe (see Demi's [1986] *Dragon Kites and Dragonflies: A Collection of Chinese Nursery Rhymes* or Agard and Nichols's [1995] *No Hickory, No Dickory, No Dock: Caribbean Nursery Rhymes*), and Stuve-Bodeen's (1998) *Elizabeti's Doll*, set in contemporary Tanzania, portrays the universal need of a small child for her own special plaything. In contrast, Kodama's (1995) *Shin's Tricycle* depicts the horror of an event that has happened only twice in human history: the dropping of the atomic bomb. We can meet new friends and develop empathy for others in books such as these.

However, children's literature often as much reflects the way childhood is viewed in a society as it provides a view into the lives of children themselves. Indeed, multiple definitions of children's literature are implied by the kinds of children's books available in different countries and cultures around the world. At the same time, commonalities also exist across cultures. A look at the status of children's literature around the world at the end of the twentieth century reveals these different and common threads.

The Status of Children's Literature around the World

One of the first universals we can find as we examine literature for children around the world is the prevalence of an oral tradition. Folklore exists in nearly every culture, sometimes in writing, but often remaining simply in oral form. In fact, in many countries where modern children's literature is nearly nonexistent, folk tales are most vibrant. For example, areas of the world such as Africa, Central and South America, the Caribbean, Asia, and the Indian subcontinent have especially rich, ancient oral traditions. India claims the world's oldest collection of stories for children, the *Panchatantra*. The tales of the Arabian Nights from the Middle East are widely known throughout the world, and many folk tales, such as "Cinderella" variants (which perhaps originated in Asia), appear in numerous cultures and have universal stature.

Within folklore, we also find many universal themes and motifs: magical transformations, the triumph of the underdog (i.e., the poorest, weakest, youngest, smallest, most physically disabled, etc.), talking animals, tricksters, the struggle between good and evil, the contrast between surface beauty and inner goodness, the quest for "happiness or lost identity" (Cullinan and Galda, 1998, p. 177), and beliefs about the origin of the world or other natural phenomena (as presented in creation stories, for example).

In many of these same areas of the world, however, indigenous literature other than folklore has lagged or is nearly absent. Much of the literature available for children was originally brought with European colonization and either published in English or translated from English into other languages. With the dominance of American and European publishing today, children's literature continues to be imported in many countries. Countries struggling with adverse economic, political, and cultural conditions simply do not have "an established infrastructure that supports and nurtures a high level of literacy" (Stan, 1999, p. 168). British author Enid Blyton, for example, was and remains one of the most popular authors worldwide. In addition, some children's books written by European settlers and set in the countries in which they lived, such as the former African colonies, contained stereotypes of native people as either savages or servants. A classic example, Edgar Rice Burroughs's *Tarzan of the Apes,* originally published in 1914, continues to perpetuate the savage native stereotype in a 1999 paperback adaptation by Robin Moore. (For further critical assessment of stereotypes portrayed today in West African children's books, see Yenika-Agbaw [1998].)

For the remainder of this section we provide an overview of children's literature by regions of the world. First, we highlight regions from which literature is less well known in the United States, such as Africa, Central and South America, the Caribbean, Asia, the Middle East, Eastern Europe, and Russia. Then we consider the more familiar literary developments in Western Europe and the English-speaking countries of Great Britain, Australia, New Zealand, and Canada.

Areas such as Africa, Latin America, and Asia are endeavoring now to produce more indigenous literature for children, but often just a few countries in each area have a relatively viable publishing presence. In many **African countries,** publishing is often limited to textbooks (Heale, 1996). Fiction, such as *Journey to Jo'burg: A South African Story* (1988) by Beverley Naidoo, is just emerging, primarily in Nigeria, Ghana, Kenya, Zimbabwe, and Namibia, with South Africa the most prolific publisher. Picture books are rare because of the prohibitive publishing cost of reproducing illustrations, although a title such as South African Niki Daly's *Not So Fast Songololo* (1986) is well-known in the United States. Many countries face obstacles, such as poor economies, low literacy rates, and multiple languages (making publishing in local languages even more costly). Thus, English-language books (in those countries colonized by Britain) continue to be prominent.

In **Central and South America and the Caribbean,** the rich mixture of traditions—American Indian, African, Chinese, and European (especially Spanish and Portuguese)—is reflected in the region's folklore (Peréz Díaz, 1996). Brazil, Argentina, Venezuela, and Cuba have the most developed children's book publishing, much of it based upon traditional literature, and have produced some outstanding authors, such as Dora Alonso from Cuba and Elsa Isabel Bonnerman from Argentina, who have achieved international recognition. Some prominent Caribbean authors, such as John Agard and Grace Nichols, are emigres to the United Kingdom or the United States. In Cuba, La Edad de Oro Award was established in the 1970s to promote children's literature. The Venezuelan publisher Ediciones Ekaré, founded in the 1980s, has some of its books, such as *The Absent-Minded Toad* by Javier Rondón (1994), distributed in the United States by Kane/Miller. However, in many countries, lack of resources has hindered development of children's book publishing.

Many **Asian countries** view children's books as secondary to textbooks. However, Japan has a highly developed literature for children (Jinguh, 1996) and is one of the few countries outside Great Britain and the United States to export its literature to other nations. Thus Japanese children's literature is among the most well-known non–English-language books for American audiences. The informational and wordless picture books of author-illustrator Mitsumasa Anno, for example, are widely available in the United States. China and India publish impressive numbers of children's books, but their quality is not yet as high as those from Japan (Jaffa, 1996; Wah & Ho, 1996). India faces the obstacle of many languages, and English-language books originating in India often predominate in the children's book market there. The Indian Children's Book Trust has led in better quality of publishing and has actively supported new writers and illustrators. A rare example of an Indian children's book available in the United States is Ruskin Bond's *Binya's Blue Umbrella* (1995), a brief novel published by Boyds Mills Press. China has eight major awards for children's books, such as the annual Children's Literary Works Award, and increasingly active support from a variety of organizations and publishers, such as the Children's Literature Research Association.

In much of the **Arab Middle East,** despite its rich folklore, there has been almost no tradition of literature specifically for children. In fact, in the past and even continuing in some places today, educators opposed folk tales as lacking educational value (Abu-Nasr, 1996). Egypt and Lebanon have the most active publishing for children, with 70% of the books published in this region coming from these two countries (Pratt & Beaty, 1999). Additionally, the Suzanne Mubarak Awards for children's books encourage writers in Egypt. However, it remains difficult for American readers to gain insights from children's books about contemporary life in this region. Although translated classics from Europe and the United States are still plentiful, indigenous **Israeli children's literature** has blossomed since the 1960s, particularly poetry, realistic fiction, and Holocaust memoirs (Shavit, 1996).

During the Soviet era in **Russia and Eastern Europe,** children's book publishing was subsidized by the state. This fostered a strong ideological influence on literature for children, but the isolation of these countries from Western European and American influences also shielded the national publishing industries from being overshadowed by foreign publishers. Although strong local traditions flourished (in folk and fairy tales, verse, and realistic fiction, for example), most of what American readers know of recent Russian children's literature has come from emigrés such as Genady Spirin, for his illustrations of folktales such as Lewis's (1994) *The Frog Princess* (Stan, 1999). From Eastern Europe, the Polish-sponsored Janusz Korczak International Literature Awards, established in 1979 to promote children's books for their humanistic values, and the Slovakian Biennale of Illustrations Bratislava (BIB), established in 1967, have kept alive international cooperation in children's literature during the Cold War era.

For much of **Europe, North America, Australia, and New Zealand,** the situation has been different. British and American publishing continues to dominate children's book markets worldwide. Such imported literature sometimes stifles local writing and publishing for children, although government subsidies in some countries, such as Norway and Canada, help to support indigenous children's literature (Stan, 1999). English-language books are widely available, and publishing of all genres of children's books in most of these countries is highly developed. Indeed, in these countries, many awards for children's literature exist that serve to promote both quality and quantity of children's book publishing.

The British Carnegie and Kate Greenaway Awards are almost as well known in the United States as the Newbery and Caldecott Medals (which are named after a famous English publisher and illustrator, respectively). A sampling of awards from other nations includes the Tir na n-Og Awards in Wales, the Reading Association of Ireland Award, the Netherlands' Theo Thijssen Award, the Lazarillo Prize and National Prize for Children's Literature in Spain, Austria's Children's Book Award of Vienna and National Children's and Juvenile Book Award, and the Crichton Award and Book Publishers' Association Best-Designed Illustrated Children's Book Award in Australia. In addition, special collections of children's literature, such as the Dromkeen in Australia and the Osborne in Canada, support the creation of and critical attention to children's literature (Stan, 1999).

Some countries are noteworthy for their historic influence on children's literature worldwide: Germany's Grimm Brothers have had a lasting impact on all European children's literature; France has some widely translated titles and authors, such as Perrault's (1697) *Tales of Times Past* or de Saint-Exupèry's (1943) *The Little Prince;* and classic tales and myths from Italy and Greece have contributed significantly to the roots of children's literature. Three other English-language countries are achieving growing international recognition for their children's book publishing: Canada, which is emerging from its traditional dependence on British and American publishing; Australia, which has had a publishing boom since the 1960s (encouraged by the national emphasis on literature-based curriculum [Stan, 1999]) and increasingly is tapping its Aboriginal heritage for literary material (Bunbury, 1996); and New Zealand, whose authors have achieved considerable global success for its size (Gilderdale, 1996). Western European countries especially advanced in children's book publishing include the Nordic countries (Finland, Norway, Sweden, and Denmark)—particularly known for their frank realism, fairy tales and fantasy; the Netherlands; and collectively Germany, Switzerland, and Austria (which collaborate in the publishing of German-language books) (Stan, 1999). In Greece, a thriving children's theater has preserved its literary heritage for children (Anagnostopoulos, 1996).

One pervasive quality of children's literature in many regions of the world is its didactic nature. Early literature for children in South America, for example, was intended to promote desirable moral values. The same is true for such countries as China and Vietnam. Political ideology also drives the content of children's books in many parts of the world: Vietnam, China, the former Soviet Union, and Eastern European countries, where proletarian ideals are or were promoted. In the early years of the Israeli state, books for children had a strongly ideological and educational purpose. In Iran, there is heavy emphasis in books for children that focus on Islamic themes and traditions. Other countries use children's literature to promote cultural or national identity and patriotism—for example, Vietnam, Malaysia, and New Zealand—and even for some European cultures, typified by a resurgence of children's books written in traditional Welsh and Irish languages.

Thus, as we enter the twenty-first century, children's literature around the world is growing, although it is more healthy in some areas than others. Folklore universally forms a strong foundation, and developing indigenous literature is beginning to replace imported European literature in many countries. Still, a few countries continue to dominate much of the children's book publishing worldwide. Finally, although didactic literature for children is widespread, in many countries, awards for children's books are raising their literary quality.

The Historical Context of International Children's Literature

There is a fairly long history of some titles crossing international boundaries, such as Spyri's (1880) *Heidi* from Switzerland, Lindgren's (1954) *Pippi Longstocking* from Sweden, and de Brunhoff's (1967) *The Story of Babar, the Little Elephant* from France, and being accepted by English-language audiences. However, reciprocity between the export of English-language books to the rest of the world and the import of non–English-language books to American audiences, in particular, has largely been absent. It is much more typical for a classic book such as Twain's (1888) *The*

Adventures of Tom Sawyer to be translated into other languages and adopted by non–English-speaking countries than for the reverse to be true. The dominance of American publishing has left little room for a perceived need for international (especially translated) children's books by readers in the United States. Since 1978, researchers have placed the number of translated children's books at around 1% in the U.S. (Tomlinson, 1998). Imports of English-language books, while greater, have also been few.

However, Hazard (1944), the noted French critic, presents a strong rationale for the importance of children's literature crossing national boundaries to promote international understanding:

> . . . children's books keep alive a sense of nationality; but they also keep alive a sense of humanity. They describe their native land lovingly, but they also describe faraway lands where unknown brothers live. They understand the essential quality of their own race; but each of them is a messenger that goes beyond mountains and rivers, beyond the seas, to the very ends of the world in search of new friendships. Every country gives and every country receives—innumerable are the exchanges—and so it comes about that in our first impressionable years the universal republic of childhood is born. (p. 146)

Since World War II, an active international children's literature movement has developed, with a woman named Jella Lepman as its primary catalyst (Tway & White, 1988). A German Jew and journalist, Lepman fled Germany during the war and became a British citizen. She returned to Germany after the war and decided to use children's literature to promote intercultural understanding in order to prevent such a devastating reoccurrence as the Nazi Holocaust. In 1948, she founded the International Youth Library (IYL) in Munich, Germany. Today the collection contains over 480,000 children's titles in more than 100 languages and is housed in a castle called Schloss Blutenburg (Martha Baker, IYL librarian, personal communication, Nov. 18, 1998). The IYL publishes *The White Ravens,* an annual selection of about 200 new titles from various countries that are recommended for translation into other languages (Tomlinson, 1998) and a traveling exhibit to the Children's Book Fair in Bologna.

Jella Lepman also founded the International Board on Books for Young People (IBBY) in 1953. This organization, headquartered in Basel, Switzerland, promotes children's literature and international understanding worldwide (IBBY Homepage: www.ibby.org). Currently, more than 60 national sections work in individual countries to promote IBBY's goals. For example, the United States Board on Books for Young People (USBBY) is the national section for the United States. Perhaps IBBY's most well-known activity is its Hans Christian Andersen award program, begun in 1956. This medal is given every two years to an author and illustrator "whose complete works have made a lasting contribution to children's literature." Nominees come from the national sections, and an international jury chooses the awardees. Uri Orlev, an author from Israel, and Lizbeth Zwerger, an illustrator from Austria, are two of the non-American winners who are perhaps more well-known to U.S. audiences. From the United States, Katherine Paterson was the 1998 winning author, and Maurice Sendak was the winning illustrator in

1970. (For a complete list of Hans Christian Andersen award recipients, see Appendix A.) Additionally, the biennial IBBY Honour List contains children's titles for writing, illustration, and translation chosen by member nations as "suitable for publication throughout the world." Nancy Farmer's (1996) *A Girl Named Disaster,* set in Zimbabwe, was a recent U.S. Honour book. The International Youth Library houses permanent collections of these book selections.

Other IBBY activities include the quarterly publication of *Bookbird: A Journal of International Children's Literature,* which includes news and articles about children's literature around the world; the Biennial Congress, an international conference on children's literature hosted by a different member country every two years; and the International Children's Book Day, held on or around Hans Christian Andersen's birthday, April 2, and sponsored by a different national section each year.

Another important development in the international children's literature movement was the establishment of the American Library Association's Mildred L. Batchelder Award. This medal honors an ALA member who promoted internationalism and the translation of children's books from other countries. The award is given annually to a United States publisher for the most outstanding

Mildred L. Batchelder

Mildred L. Batchelder is the namesake of the award honoring the most outstanding books originally published in a foreign country, then translated and published in the United States. This remarkable woman was born in 1901 in Lynn, Massachusetts, and she died at the age of 96 in 1998 after a long career as the premier children's librarian in the United States. Batchelder graduated from Mt. Holyoke College and the New York State University Library School in Albany. She served as director of the children's department at the Omaha, Nebraska, Public Library and as a school librarian in Evanston, Illinois, before joining the staff of the American Library Association in 1936.

At ALA, Batchelder led the School and Children's Library Division and then became executive secretary of both the Children's Services Division and the Young Adult Services Division, a position she held until her retirement in 1966. These divisions are now known as the Association for Library Service to Children and the Young Adult Services Association. Her leadership at ALA is recognized and

highly respected. In Batchelder's obituary for the *Horn Book,* Zena Sutherland (1999) wrote, "Mildred was an ardent and articulate advocate not only of the publication of books from other countries but also for the use of audiovisual materials and for the defense of intellectual freedom" (p. 100).

Batchelder received many awards and honors, such as the Constance Lindsay Skinner Award of the Women's National Book Association and Chicago Children's Reading Round Table Award. She was the subject of a 1981 doctoral dissertation by Dorothy Jean Anderson at Texas Woman's University entitled, "Mildred L. Batchelder: A Study of Leadership." In addition, she was named an honorary member of the Board of Trustees of the International Youth Library in recognition of her commitment to the international exchange of children's literature.

The American Library Association's web page highlights Mildred Batchelder's work and her life's commitment to "eliminate barriers to understanding between people of different cultures, races, nations, and languages."

English-translated children's book of the year. Batchelder viewed books as good-will ambassadors among cultures and stated:

> When children of one country come to know and love the books and stories of many countries, they have made an important beginning towards international under-standing. To know the classic stories of a country creates a climate, an attitude for understanding the people for whom the literature is a heritage. When children know they are reading, in translation, the same stories which children in another country are reading, a sense of nearness grows and expands. Interchange of children's books between countries, through translations, influences communication between the peoples of those countries, and if the books chosen for travel from language to lan-guage are worthy books, the resulting communication may be deeper, richer, more sympathetic, more enduring. I accept and believe these assumptions. (1966, p. 34)

Uri Orlev also has been a three-time Batchelder Award recipient for *The Lady with the Hat* (1995), *The Man from the Other Side* (1991), and *The Island on Bird Street* (1984), all translated from Hebrew. Other recent winners have included *The Friends* by Kazumi Yumoto (1996), translated from Japanese, and *The Robber and Me* by Josef Holub (1997), translated from German. (For a complete listing of Batchelder Award titles, see Appendix B.)

International book fairs also promote the exchange of children's literature among countries, by bringing together publishers, editors, and literary agents "to negotiate publishing and licensing rights for foreign publication" (Tomlinson, 1998, p. 18). The Children's Book Fair in Bologna, Italy, the Frankfurt (Germany) Bookfair, and the Zimbabwe International Book Fair held in Harare are major annual exhibitions. Since 1967, the Biennale of Illustrations Bratislava (BIB), held every two years in cooperation by the Slovak Republic Ministry of Culture, the United Nations Educational, Scientific and Cultural Organization (UNESCO), and IBBY, is the largest juried international competition for excellence in children's book illustration (Stottele, 1997). A display of the current Hans Christian Andersen illustrator recipient's work is featured at the competition.

UNESCO engages in a variety of programs to promote writing, illustrating, and publishing of children's books, particularly in countries where little is done. For example, the Asia/Pacific Cultural Centre for UNESCO has operated a Cop-ublication Programme since 1971 in which children's books are "first published in English as a master edition and then each country publishes vernacular language versions in local publishing houses" (ACCU homepage: www.accu.or.jp/book/acp/index.htm). Another UNESCO/ACCU-sponsored program is the Noma Concours for Picture Book Illustrations. Similar to the BIB, this is a biennial competition established in 1978 to encourage illustrators in Asia and the Pacific, Latin America and the Caribbean, Africa, and the Arab States. Finally, ACCU also offers workshops and seminars to support writers, illustrators, and publishers of children's books in developing countries.

Copublication in the United States is a relatively recent development. Some-times this involves publishers from different countries arranging to publish each other's books, as done by Farrar, Straus and Giroux in the United States and the Swedish publisher, Rabén and Sjögren (Tomlinson, 1998) for Björk's (1987) *Lin-nea in Monet's Garden*, for example. Boyds Mills Press publishes titles, such as

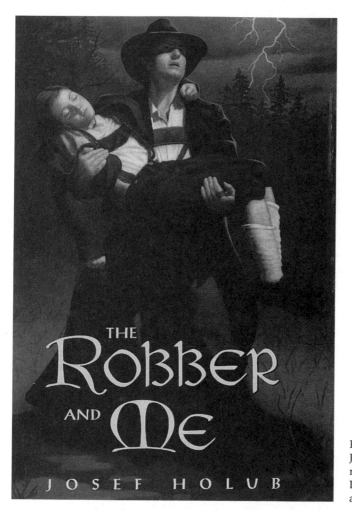

From: *The Robber and Me* by Josef Holub. Jacket illustration by Dave Kramer; copyright, © 1997 by Henry Holt and Company, LLC. Reprinted by permission of Henry Holt and Company, LLC

Madoulina: A Girl Who Wanted to Go to School by Joël Eboueme Bognomo (1999), from Aile Cameroun in the African country of Cameroon. Some companies are multinational as is North-South Books, the American imprint of Nord-Süd Verlag titles from Switzerland. Perhaps its best-known publication is Marcus Pfister's (1992) *The Rainbow Fish*. Originally, Nord-Süd books were distributed by Henry Holt, as Kane/Miller does now in the United States for Spanish-language titles from Ediciones Ekaré of Venezuela. In fact, a growing number of publishers, who either produce original titles with international settings or who import (and often translate) children's books from other countries, are accessible to American audiences. (For a list of these publishers, see Appendix C.)

Thus, today there is a burgeoning international children's literature movement on several fronts. The diverse organizations promoting the movement and variations in publishing just described bring us finally to the question of how to define international children's literature.

Defining International Children's Literature

In his book, *Children's Books from Other Countries*, Tomlinson (1998) defines international children's literature as "that body of books originally published for children in a country other than the United States in a language of that country and later published in this country" (p. 4). He specifically excludes books "originally published in the United States for children of this country but whose characters or settings are foreign" (p. 4). Thus, he includes Arno Bohlmeijer's (1996) *Something Very Sorry*, originally published in the Netherlands, but not *The Distant Talking Drum* (1995), a poetry collection originally published in the United States and written by Nigerian emigré, Isaac Olaleye.

On the other hand, Tway and White (1988) state that ". . . the international experience is available in books and can take many routes: choosing books published abroad in a shared language and now released for sale in one's own country; selecting books in translation that reflect other cultures; finding books published in the native country that are about other countries; and looking for universal motifs or archetypes . . . " (p. 179). Finally, Pratt and Beaty (1999) use the term "transcultural children's literature," defined as, "children's books that portray peoples, cultures, and geographic regions of the world that exist outside the reader's own country" (p. 2).

For the purposes of this book, we have chosen to define international children's literature as books written and published first in countries other than the United States (both in English and in translation), books written by immigrants to the United States about their home countries and published in the United States, books written by authors from countries other than the United States but originally published in the United States, and books written by American authors and published in the United States with settings in other countries. Thus, we include books such as Almagor's (1995) *Under the Domim Tree* originally published in Israel, Chinese immigrant Ji-Li Jiang's (1997) *Red Scarf Girl: A Memoir of the Cultural Revolution*, Deborah Turney Zagwÿn's (1999) *Apple Batter* (a book published in the United States by a Canadian author), and Jane Kurtz's (1998) *The Storyteller's Beads*, written by an American author and set in Ethiopia. While we note when books have bilingual editions, such as Torres's (1995) *Saturday Sancocho* in English and Spanish, we do not include books available in the United States only in other languages. We also do not include multicultural literature that portrays racial, ethnic, religious, or cultural groups within the United States. An alternative term we will use to describe the literature we examine in this book is "global literature."

We acknowledge that our definition of international literature is restricted to that available in the United States and does not "represent a microcosm of the greater world of international children's literature" (Stan, 1999, p. 168), much of which never appears in this country. Even books originally published abroad will likely undergo changes, such as altering the size to fit American presses or the content and illustrations to make them more suitable for American audiences and less culturally specific. However, as noted in this chapter, Hazard (1944) and Batchelder (1966) make a compelling case for the importance of international children's literature in spite of these limitations. In the next chapter, we detail a specific rationale for the value and importance of a global perspective in children's literature.

CHAPTER

2

The Value and Importance of International Children's Literature

Brightly painted plants and animals cover an oversized piece of paper as children in a second-grade classroom create a mural of the rain forest. They have also written essays on "How I Can Save the Rain Forest," which are displayed on a bulletin board. Children's books about rain forests in different parts of the world are found in the reading center. These books include such titles as Keister's (1995) *Fernando's Gift*, a bilingual picture book about a young boy in the Costa Rican rain forest, and Olaleye's (1998) *Lake of the Big Snake*, a picture book about two friends living in a Nigerian rain forest village.

In another school, a fourth-grade class is immersed in the study of Australia. After the class generated a KWL chart, they enthusiastically began researching answers to the questions for the "What we want to know" column. Their efforts resulted in a class museum with artifacts about Australia and a celebration of Australian life complete with food, music, and games. Books such as Wheatley and Rawlins's (1989) *My Place*, an Australian informational book that traces a tract of land from the present day back in time 200 years, and Reynolds's (1992) *Down Under*, a contemporary photo-essay about the Tiwi aborigines, supported the children's inquiry. Daily the teacher reads aloud to the class chapters from the award-winning Australian novel by Park (1984) *Playing Beatie Bow*, a time travel story set in both modern-day Sydney and Australia in the 1880s.

Introduction

These classroom vignettes reflect teachers who are committed to the importance of sharing the world with their students. In the interdisciplinary rain forest unit, children are developing important concepts that relate to conservation, ecology, and natural resources. In the second classroom, the teacher has selected a specific continent, Australia, as a setting in which to explore aspects of culture and to encourage students to generate their own questions about life in another society. Today's world is shrinking due to global communications and increased mobility. Technology now instantaneously links children around the world to each other, and many have the opportunity to travel widely to other countries and/or have family ties to places outside their home countries. Yet, at the same time, ethnic and cultural divides seem to be widening. Daily, children see on television vivid images of suffering and war. They witness the plight of children like themselves who are refugees from oppression, violence, and harsh economic conditions. An important role of education is to foster children's understanding and appreciation for others so that they can actively participate as citizens in a global community.

Further, the population of the United States is becoming increasingly diverse. In addition to children of immigrants from European countries and children born in the United States of parallel cultures such as Native American, African American, Asian American, and Latino/a, the current wave of immigration brings individuals from Africa, Asia, the Caribbean, and Central America. Between 1980 and 1990 over 8.9 million legal immigrants entered the United States. Of these, 49% were from North and South America while 38% were from Asia and the Pacific. Children's understanding of these cultures enables them to develop positive peer relationships. The traditions and heritage of cultures around the world enrich the lives of all. Children's literature with a global perspective is an appropriate, interesting, and enjoyable way for students to gain knowledge and understanding.

You may wonder why an elementary teacher in the United States should incorporate international children's literature into the curriculum. In particular, why should children be exposed to literature about other countries beyond the literature about the many cultures already represented in the United States? The answer to this question is fundamentally the same as to why children's literature should be an integral part of every child's school experience. As Charlotte Huck (1989) has so eloquently expressed:

> Through literature, children can begin to develop a sense of their humanness; they can develop new insights into the behavior of others and themselves. Literature can add a new dimension to life and create a new awareness, a greater sensitivity to people and surroundings. It can educate the heart as well as the head. (p. 262)

In addition, children's literature with a global perspective offers some unique benefits for children. These benefits can be approached from two perspectives: the value of these books for children's growth and development and the books' positive relationship to specific curricular connections.

Benefits to Children

As with all literature, international children's literature can spark the imagination, nurture curiosity, and delight the heart and mind. Children in the elementary years are open to learning about the world around them. They are rapidly developing in all areas: cognitively, socially, and morally. Elementary children are in a constant process of constructing their understanding of the physical, social, and cultural aspects of the world in which they live. Exposure to international children's literature can support all aspects of children's development. In reviewing relevant research, Evans (1987) concluded that "research indicates that elementary students are not only developmentally ready but that this might be an especially important age to include global concepts in the curriculum" (p. 548).

Children's literacy development during the elementary years is rapidly expanding as they independently read, write, and understand how spoken and written language works. Through stories—listening to them, reading them, and writing them—children are connected with peers around the world who also enjoy hearing, reading, and writing stories. Dyson and Genishi (1994) attest to the importance of story: "Through stories by children, teachers, and professional authors, characters—given life through word pictures and verbal rhythms—enter the classroom, and in so doing they bring new experiences and points of view" (p. 5). Unforgettable international characters have indeed entered American classrooms. Pippi Longstocking entertains us from Sweden, Charlie and his chocolate factory visit us from England, and Anne Frank inspires us from Holland. Through stories, both fictional and true, children learn about people, places, and events in all corners of the globe.

Such learning can increase international understanding and help to remove barriers among people. As Hazel Rochman (1993) explains:

> A good book can help to break down these barriers. Books can make a difference in dispelling prejudice and building community; not with role models and literal recipes, not with noble messages about the human family, but with enthralling stories that make us imagine the lives of others. A good story lets you know people as individuals in all their particularity and conflict; and once you see someone as a person—flawed, complex, striving—then you've reached beyond stereotype. Stories, writing them, telling them, sharing them, transforming them, enrich us and connect us and help us know each other. (p. 19)

Literature from around the world supports children's language development. As children are exposed to books based in varied languages, they construct knowledge about the structures of other languages, the distinctive sounds of languages, and the unique vocabulary. Often books will incorporate vocabulary of another language. In *My Freedom Trip* by Park and Park (1998), two sisters tell the true story of their mother's escape from North to South Korea. Various Korean words such as Apa (father) and yut (a Korean board game) are used throughout the text. Through reading this book, children also increase their English vocabularies with words that relate to the Korean culture such as rice paddies, pagoda roofs, and barley tea. In addition, Korean characters, which are explained at the beginning of the book, appear on each page, thus exposing children to another written language. This book could serve as a springboard for a comparative mini-unit on the written symbols that represent different languages.

Bilingual texts help children see that a story can be conveyed in more than one language. In Delgado's (1996) picture book, *Chave's memories=Los recuerdos de Chave,* a woman recalls her childhood visits to her grandparents' home in Mexico.

My Freedom Trip

A Child's Escape from North Korea

by Frances Park and Ginger Park
Illustrated by Debra Reid Jenkins

Jacket illustration copyright © 1998 by Debra Reid Jenkins from *My Freedom Trip* by Frances Park and Ginger Park. Used with permission of Boyds Mills Press.

Each double-page spread features the text, printed in both Spanish and English, on the left side and a colorful, full-page, realistic painting on the right. The English and Spanish text are separated by a smaller painting that features an aspect of the full-page illustration. For example, the text begins: "Oh, how special it was to visit my grandparents' ranch, La Burrita, in Mexico" (unpaged). The text continues with a short paragraph followed by a painting of two pieces of luggage. At the lower portion of the page is the Spanish text: "Qué especial para nosotros era ir al rancho La Burrita de mis abuelitos en México" (unpaged).

The beauty of language is universally appreciated through the rhythms, rhymes and images of poetry. Rich sounds and cadences of a language can be experienced through reading poetry from other lands aloud. Poetry books from the Caribbean such as Joseph's (1990) *Coconut Kind of Day* set in Trinidad and Gunning's (1998) *Under the Breadfruit Tree* set in Jamaica feature the distinctive language patterns and vocabulary of these island nations where different dialects of English are spoken. Learning about other languages and dialects is an enriching experience that enhances our understanding of other cultures.

International children's books can support the development of students' visual literacy as they read the illustrations and photographs in books. Illustrations help establish the setting of the story, reveal aspects of daily life in a culture, and include cultural conventions. For instance, Ted Lewin's (1995) watercolor illustrations for *Sacred River* bring readers to the shores of the Ganges River as it flows through Benares, India. Readers see pilgrims cleansing themselves and making flower offerings. Cultures also have distinctive artistic motifs and styles. Kiefer (1995) discusses how artists incorporate cultural conventions in their work. She points out that "the theme of the book, its setting in time and place, and its overall effect is strengthened by the artist's choice of certain historical or cultural conventions" (p. 138). She notes the example of contemporary illustrators who have been influenced by techniques of Chinese art such as Demi's (1991) paintings for *Chingis Khan*.

British educator Penni Cotton (1999) reports the effectiveness of picture books in facilitating university students' communication when they work with children in other countries. She indicates that "sharing picture books became an entrée into the children's world for many students. Spoken language did not appear to be a barrier; indeed, it was the visual narratives of these well-chosen books and the universality of themes that enables these texts to become a catalyst within the communication process" (p. 18). Such books should have the same effect on children from different countries, who may speak different languages. In addition to paintings, drawings, and mixed media found in picture books, many contemporary informational books are illustrated with color photographs that enable children to travel around the globe, experience a culture firsthand, and enter into the daily lives of children in other parts of the world. *Wake Up, World! A Day in the Life of Children Around the World* by Hollyer (1999) follows the day of eight children from the United Kingdom, United States, Brazil, Ghana, Russia, Vietnam, Australia, and India. Through color photographs and text we see each child waking up, starting the day, going off to school, and participating in other daily experiences. After reading this book, children in small groups can research the life of a child in another country and describe that child's day in the same format as *Wake Up, World!*

In the elementary years, children's social and emotional development undergoes a shift in emphasis as children's perspective-taking ability increases and they more easily consider the needs and thoughts of others. During this time, children empathize with the feelings of others and therefore identify in many ways with children like themselves who live around the globe. International literature can indeed foster children's development of empathy. Australian journalist Allan Baillie (1995) discusses the evolution of *Little Brother* (1992), the realistic novel about 11-year-old Vuthy living in Cambodia in 1969 during Pol Pot's "reign of terror" (p. 148). He points out his desire to write a book "about a child's view of Cambodia for children" (p. 152) and notes that "I was writing *Little Brother* to make a boy from Utah feel he could be the boy in Cambodia. By a casual spin of the coin" (p. 154).

As they read about boys and girls from other lands, children come to recognize the similarities that bind all peoples together. Regardless of where they live in the world, children share the same needs, wants, interests, and feelings. Young children in the United States laugh at books their peers in other countries also enjoy. Humorous picture books such as Burningham's (1971) *Mr. Gumpy's Outing* from Great Britain abound in countries around the world. This cumulative tale about Mr. Gumpy, his animal friends, and their ill-fated outing has been enjoyed by children for more than a quarter-century. A contemporary cumulative tale, Kharms's (1996) *First Second* from Russia, describes a young person's hilarious journey and the travelers he encounters. Children will delight at Rondón's (1994) *The Absent-Minded Toad,* a picture book from Venezuela about a toad who goes to market but forgets to buy anything. Such humorous books lend themselves to dramatization, with children reenacting the events of a story.

At the same time, children can develop an appreciation for differences, both cultural and individual, which make each of us a unique person. Lynch-Brown and Tomlinson (1993) point out that one value of international literature is that "children are given an opportunity to enjoy the best-loved stories of their peers around the world. This, in turn, can help students develop a bond of shared experience with children of other nations and acquire cultural literacy with a global perspective" (p. 182). Increased knowledge about others and appreciation of difference will begin to dispel stereotypes we have of people from other cultures. In discussing the motivation for writing *The Day of Ahmed's Secret* by Heide and Gilliland (1990), a picture book about a young boy in Cairo, Egypt, Judith Gilliland (1995) describes that she and her coauthor mother "hoped to counteract the awful stereotypes of Arabs that children are presented with in many and subtle ways in cartoons, in sitcoms, in comic books, even in commercials" (p. 107).

In addition to social development, children's moral development is also undergoing a major shift. In terms of Kohlberg's stages of moral development, children in the elementary years are usually in stage 2: the instrumental purpose orientation. Children in this stage are very concerned with issues of fairness and therefore are at an appropriate age to discuss books that present moral dilemmas. Such discussions promote children's growth of moral reasoning. With such topics as apartheid, war, prejudice, and peer relationships, international books present a multitude of moral and ethical dilemmas and issues for children to discuss. Protagonists in novels often face difficult decisions and dilemmas. Children can discuss these decisions and generate other solutions and alternative responses. In *No Turning Back: A Novel of South Africa* by Naidoo (1997), Sipho, the 12-year-old main character, faces many decisions as he runs away from an abusive stepfather, lives on the streets of Johannesburg with other homeless boys, and tries to find the place where he belongs. Sipho's struggles and the choices he makes will no doubt prompt much discussion among older children.

Children's critical thinking can also be fostered as they explore multiple perspectives on people, places, and ideas in books. Children can compare books on a similar topic that reflect different points of view or they can compare the treatment of a topic in different genres of literature. For example, primary-aged children can learn about the Tuareg, a nomadic people of the Sahara Desert, through both an informational book and picture storybook. Beautiful color photographs support the text in Reynolds's (1991) *Sahara*, which introduces the Tuareg culture and lifestyle through the perspective of Manda, a young boy. Similarly, Kessler's (1995b) picture storybook, *One Night: A Story from the Desert* tells a story about the boy Muhammed in a fictionalized first-person account. Children can compare and contrast the aspects of Tuareg life and culture that are presented in these different genres. Children can also compare the treatment of a similar theme as it is developed in different settings. For example, interracial/ethnic friendship is explored in contemporary novels like Gordon's (1987) *Waiting for the Rain*, set in South Africa, and Schami's (1990) *A Hand Full of Stars*, set in Damascus, Syria. The protagonists of both books are adolescent males who live in turbulent times for their countries. As they read and dialogue about these novels, children can explore how the social and political context influences the boys' relationships.

In summary, international literature enhances children's language and literacy development, their visual literacy, and their critical thinking skills. It also can support children's social, emotional, and moral growth as they identify with characters in books, recognize similarities and differences, and develop empathy for children around the globe.

Curricular and Instructional Benefits

International children's books not only foster children's individual growth and development, they also serve as a powerful medium to support many areas of the elementary curriculum. In addition to relating to specific subjects such as social studies, current events, and reading/language arts, books are critical to teaching and learning in interdisciplinary curriculum approaches such as theme teaching, global education, multicultural education, and Holocaust education. Children visit other parts of the world and grow in their knowledge of specific facts and in their understanding of various concepts as they read books from and about other countries. International books expand and enhance children's perspectives about people, places, and ideas.

Curricular Links

Books can augment the content of the traditional social studies curriculum—history, geography, economics, citizenship, cultures, and communities. Oden (1992) points out how children's literature can foster such geography concepts as location, place, human-environment interactions, movement, and regions. She specifically mentions Lewin's (1983) *Jafta—The Journey* set in South Africa as dealing with location and Heide and Gilliland's (1990) *The Day of Ahmed's Secret* as supporting several geographic concepts. Historical fiction provides young readers with a lens of the past through which to understand modern societies they may be studying. Sutcliffe's (1990) *The Shining Company* takes readers back to Great Britain in 600 A.D., and Conlon-McKenna's (1990) *Under the Hawthorne Tree* provides insights into the Irish potato famine of the 1840s.

Another curricular area is current events. One only has to open the daily newspaper to recognize the importance to children of better understanding and appreciating others. Conflicts of all kinds divide people over racial, cultural, religious, and economic differences. In addition, global issues, such as poverty and environmental degradation, concern us all. Children's perspectives on current issues, as well as the background children need in order to make sense of them, may be found in books. The conflict in the Balkans is documented from a child's perspective in *Zlata's Diary: A Child's Life in Sarajevo* by Filipovic (1994). It is the actual diary of 11-year-old Zlata, whose first entry is September, 1991, before her native city became a war zone and last diary entry is October 17, 1993, during shelling of her city. Children in the United States can follow how the life of a child, much like their own, changed dramatically because of a contemporary war.

In the area of reading/language arts, international children's literature supports the study of literature and the development of literary understanding. Children's knowledge about the universality of literature, the range of world literature, and culturally derived characteristics of literature can be expanded. Through international books, literary elements such as character development, setting, universal literary themes, and author's craft can be explored. Many of the great, beloved classics of children's literature have been written in languages other than English and in countries other than the United States. *Heidi* was originally written in German and is set in Switzerland while Carlo Collodi's *The Adventures of Pinocchio* (1891/1988) is from Italy. In addition, the roots of modern literature are found in folklore from around the world. Grimms' fairy tales, Aesop's fables, and Greek and Roman myths are part of our literary heritage and alluded to by countless authors throughout the ages. Often, knowledge of this literary heritage enhances understanding and appreciation of contemporary literature. As students are exposed to literature from all genres written by authors around the world, they are provided powerful models for their own writing. For instance, the Japanese poetry form, haiku, has become popular in elementary classrooms for children to emulate in their own poetry writing. Students can consult Gollub's (1998) *Cool Melons—Turn to Frogs!* which features the life and haiku poems of Issa, the eighteenth-century Japanese poet, to further their understanding of this poetic form.

Integrated themes of study can also incorporate a global perspective with books from around the world supporting concept development. For example, if a primary teacher were focusing on the theme, "All Kinds of Families," she could share a variety of books set and written around the world about children and their families. Nigerian native Ifeoma Onyefulu describes the ogbo, or age group, which serves as an extended family for children in Nigerian villages. In the photo-essay, *Ogbo: Sharing Life in an African Village* (1996), Onyefulu describes the importance of the ogbo in the culture of the village and in the lives of the children. In the picture book, *The Mats,* Philippine author Francisco Arcellana (1999) recounts the loving relationship of a father to his family as Papa has brought each family member a special mat. Children may discuss the similarities and differences between these families and their own.

Reprinted with permission of Harcourt, Inc. © 1996.

In the upper elementary grades, a classroom may study the theme of journeys and explore the multiple meanings of this concept and how it also serves as a metaphor for other ideas. In *Year of Impossible Goodbyes* by Choi (1991), 10-year-old Sooken lives in North Korea during World War II. Sooken, with her younger brother and their mother, undertakes a perilous journey to join her father in South Korea. Similarly, 11-year-old Nhamo escapes an arranged marriage in Mozambique and sets out on a journey to Zimbabwe in search of her father in Farmer's (1996) *A Girl Named Disaster.* The parallels between the lives of these two girls and the journeys they undertake, as well as the differences in the purposes, contexts, and settings of their journeys, will provide rich material for student discussion and written response.

Links to Global Education

Almost 25 years ago, Robert G. Hanvey (1976) wrote what now is considered the classic framework for global education. He set forth five dimensions of global education: perspective consciousness, "State of the Planet" awareness, cross-cultural awareness, knowledge of global dynamics, and awareness of human choices. Kniep (1986) further elaborated the content of global education as follows:

> I propose four elements of study as being essential and basic to a global education: the study of human values, the study of global systems, the study of global problems and issues, and the study of the history of contacts and interdependence among peoples, cultures, and nations. (p. 437)

Children's literature can support the development of these dimensions and content through the rich array of books in all genres from around the world.

As noted by Kniep (1986) and others, interdependence among peoples of the world is a key concept in global education. Through modern communications, the media, technology, and increased mobility, the world is smaller and increasingly interdependent. UNICEF Canada sponsored a curriculum development project on using children's literature as a means to understand the developing world (Diakiw, 1990). One of the units focused specifically on global interdependence and selected books that "make provocative reading and raise critical questions about the way in which we relate to economically less fortunate countries" (p. 299).

Books can help children understand such global issues as ecology, poverty, natural disaster, economic development, and health. Merryfield and White (1996) identify global issues to be studied in five areas: political issues such as human rights, cultural/social issues such as refugees, development issues such as poverty, economic issues such as transportation, and environmental issues such as pollution. For example, *Out of the Dump* by Franklin and McGirr (1996), which features the writings and photographs of children living in the garbage dump of Guatemala City, Guatemala, relates to the issue of poverty as well as to the cultural/social issue of homelessness. Kessler's (1995a) *All the King's Animals: The Return of Endangered Wildlife to Swaziland,* a photo-essay about conservationist Ted

Reilly, who worked to reintroduce native wildlife to Swaziland, focuses on the environmental issue of endangered species.

Links to Multicultural Education

Global education is closely related to multicultural education. Diaz, Massialas, and Xanthopoulos (1999) point out that both fields include the "study of cultural diversity, human rights, varied curricular perspectives and prejudice reduction" (p. 3). Although these two curricular emphases share several features, there are also differences between them. While both focus on aspects of culture, global education deals with cultures outside the United States in countries around the world. Multicultural education, on the other hand, concentrates on parallel cultures within the United States. According to Banks (1999), multicultural education is "an educational reform movement whose major goal is to restructure curricula and educational institutions so that students from diverse social-class, racial, and ethnic groups—as well as both gender groups—will experience equal educational opportunities" (p. 116). The two areas of study, global and multicultural education, can support each other. Banks points out that "citizens who have an understanding of and empathy for the cultures within their own nation are probably more likely to function effectively in cultures outside of their nation than are citizens who have little understanding of and empathy for cultures within their own society" (pp. 23–24). The reverse should be equally true.

Children's books can support this relationship between global and multicultural education. For instance, in order to understand the experience of the Hmong people in the United States, children would benefit from knowing about the unique history of this refugee group. A teacher may share *The Whispering Cloth: A Refugee's Story* by Shea (1995), a fictional picture book based on the Hmong experience in the Ban Vinai refugee camp in Thailand. Here Mai's grandmother teaches her how to stitch a traditional story cloth, which Mai does to tell her own story. This book can be paired with the informational picture book by Cha, *Dia's Story Cloth: The Hmong People's Journey of Freedom* (1996), written by a Hmong woman who came to the United States when she was 15 years old. It also features a story cloth that explains the Hmong's history and emigration to the United States. From these two books, children can list facts and information that they learned about the Hmong. They can also create a personal story cloth to tell about their own family history.

Another link between global education and multicultural education involves the comparison of the experience of parallel cultures in the United States with those in locations around the world. For example, the experience of Japanese Americans during World War II can be compared to that of Japanese living in other parts of the world at that time. In the award-winning novel by Salisbury, *Under the Blood-Red Sun* (1994), Tomikazu is a happy 13-year-old who loves baseball and lives in Hawaii. When Japan bombs Pearl Harbor in 1941, his life radically changes. Similarly, Yoko is a Japanese girl living in northern Korea. As World War II escalates and Japan invades Korea, the danger to Yoko and her family heighten in Watkins's *So Far From the Bamboo Grove* (1994). Multiple perspectives on war, prejudice, and problem solving can be examined as children respond to these books through oral discussion, written expression, and artistic creations.

Links to Holocaust Education

Holocaust Education provides an awareness of the Holocaust, the planned and systematic extermination of over six million Jews and five million non-Jews (gypsies, homosexuals, political prisoners, and the disabled) by the Nazi regime during World War II. The lessons we have learned from the Holocaust resonate today as our world struggles with prejudice, discrimination, and racial cleansing. Many states have developed Holocaust education curriculum. The United States Holocaust Council is mandated by Congress to provide Holocaust education materials and staff development programs for teachers.

In recent years, there has been a proliferation of children's books about the Holocaust for children of all ages in a range of genres including picture books, memoirs, informational books, and historical novels. Teachers have written about their positive experiences in sharing Holocaust literature with children (Tunnell & Ammon, 1993; Zack, 1991). Such books have been written in varied countries and provide multiple perspectives on this event. For instance, picture books present a personal picture of the Holocaust, oftentimes from a child's perspective—both Jewish and non-Jewish. Originally published in France, the award-winning picture book by Hoestlandt, *Star of Fear, Star of Hope* (1995), focuses on the friendship of Helen and her Jewish friend, Lydia, who is required to always wear a yellow star. The story, geared for children ages 7 to 10, explores the thoughts and feelings of Helen, who narrates this fictional story in the first person and who as a child felt confusion and anger toward Lydia who had to leave Helen's birthday party in haste due to approaching danger. Similary, Wild's Australian picture book, *Let the Celebrations Begin!* (1991), is a fictionalized first-person account based on a true incident. As the concentration camp inmates await liberation, they make toys from old scraps to prepare for their celebration. These picture books for younger children present one small incident from the Holocaust and its effect on a child.

Many fine historical novels have been written in other countries and translated into English. These novels provide varied perspectives of World War II as seen through the eyes of children and young adults in other countries. Set in Holland and translated from the Dutch, *Hide and Seek* by Vos (1991) presents a fictionalized account of the author's life in hiding during the Nazi occupation of her country. The Batchelder–award-winning novel, *The Boys from St. Petri* by Reuter (1994), translated from the Danish, is a fast-paced story about the bravery of Danish youth in resisting the Nazi invasion of their country.

In recent years, first-person memoirs written for upper elementary and middle school children have increased as the public desire for survivors to tell their stories has become apparent. These memoirs focus on the remembrances of adults who were children during the Holocaust and are set in various countries throughout Europe. Many of these books have received awards for their literary merit, such as Lobel's *No Pretty Pictures* (1998) and Wassiljewa's *Hostage to War* (1997). Anita Lobel, the well-known children's book illustrator, recounts her childhood in Nazi-occupied Poland, her life in Sweden immediately following liberation, and her eventual immigration to the United States. Tatjana Wassiljewa, in a book originally written in Russian and translated into English, describes her experiences growing up in the Soviet Union during the war.

Informational books provide historical background and factual material regarding World War II and the Holocaust. Anne Frank's life continues to be of high interest to children. A recent informational book, *Anne Frank, Beyond the Diary* by van der Rol and Verhoeven (1992), was originally published in the Netherlands and provides a photographic essay on Anne Frank's life and the times in which she lived. British journalist Michael Leapman (1998) chronicles the lives of eight children including a gypsy, a Polish boy taken by the Nazis to a Hitler Youth Camp, and a German Jewish girl who was sent on the Kindertransporte to England in *Witnesses to War*.

Holocaust studies can also be enhanced through poetry. The children incarcerated at the Terezín concentration camp in Czechoslovakia participated in secret school instruction and created drawings and poems that have been collected into *. . . I Never Saw Another Butterfly . . .* by Volavková (1993). Jo Hall, a teacher in Worthington, Ohio, who engages her fifth- and sixth-grade students in a study of the Holocaust, asks them to express their reflections through poetry. These poems reflect a sophisticated level of intensity and depth of thought. Students yearly share their poems with school board and community members, and the teacher compiles them into a class book. The following poem was written by an 11-year-old student in her class:

The Holocaust

There was a man who hated the Jews
He wouldn't feel that way if he were in their shoes
He killed them all and made them flee
But there was something he couldn't see
The Jews had courage beyond belief
And kept their hope as they fought their grief
This man hurt the young and killed the old
He beat the weak and scared the bold
Hitler was this man's name
He frightened all and drove many insane
No one stood up to this man of hate
A master race he wanted to create
But soon it was all too late
The world was a giant field of sadness
A sphere of hate, a place of madness
At last, the hurting ended
All the killing and hating descended
We learn about this event today
And I would just like to say
Everyone should be treated equal
For this tragic story must not have a sequel

*By Brinn Acker**

*Reprinted with permission of Suzanne Acker, mother.

Conclusion

International children's books benefit children in multiple ways and also provide strong links to all aspects of the curriculum. When teachers share these books with their students, they bring the world into their classrooms and open up limitless opportunities for discussion and response. Through international books children meet peers in other lands, visit new locations, travel back in history, and learn about contemporary people, animals, events, and places. The next chapter discusses some issues surrounding international children's literature that both teachers and readers need to consider.

3 Issues in International Children's Literature

As amply demonstrated, we hope, in the previous chapter, there are many compelling reasons to have and use global children's literature in our contemporary world. However, whenever we cross cultural boundaries, certain issues also arise. Some of these are the same considerations that relate to multicultural literature, such as authenticity and the insider-outsider perspective, but there are additional concerns with international literature. For educators and critics, the relevant issues are: availability, authenticity, translation, publication, and selection and evaluation. In many instances, these considerations overlap with each other.

Availability of Global Children's Literature

First, the availability of children's literature in the United States from or about a particular country or region of the world may depend upon the number of immigrants from that area in the United States, how much attention that area is getting currently in the mass media, and even the status or acceptance of a particular culture in the United States (Pratt & Beaty, 1999). For example, as immigration patterns change, publishing trends may mirror those patterns, as seen in the relatively large number of bilingual English/Spanish books now available to accompany the influx and growing political power of Latina/o immigrants. Yet, most of these books are set in the United States, rather than in the immigrants' native countries, and books portraying Asian cultures are relatively prevalent because of the generally positive status many of those groups enjoy. In contrast, the Arab world often has been portrayed less favorably in U.S. media, and literature about Arab cultures has correspondingly less prominence and quantity. History and timeliness also direct attention toward certain types of literature. For example, as many Holocaust survivors age, their stories are appearing in print in increasing numbers. Finally, for economic reasons that will be explored later, imported English-language books from Britain, Canada, Australia, or New Zealand are much more likely to be available in the U.S. market than are translated books.

Another issue is the kind of literature available from and about other countries. As noted in Chapter 1, folklore is virtually universal to every culture, while other types of literature are severely limited in many areas. Perhaps because of this, and also because of other issues such as publication rights, translation, or even authenticity, folklore constitutes much of global literature. Such heavy reliance on traditional literature does not provide a balanced view of contemporary life around the world. It may, however, give insight about beliefs and values that continue to shape cultures today, as well as commonalities across cultures. In addition to folklore, other genres provide readers with a more well-rounded perspective of life in other countries: Picture books, through words and pictures, depict both content and art; realistic fiction offers the opportunity to "live" in other cultures through characters created; fantasy explores the universal world of imagination; informational books and biography provide knowledge about unfamiliar people and places; and poetry introduces the nuances and rhythm of language and imagery.

When availability of a wide range of literature is lacking, readers may gain misconceptions and stereotypes about other regions. For example, books with generic African settings can create the impression of the continent as an undifferentiated area (or even as a single country) by obscuring the wide diversity—geographically, politically, culturally, socially, ethnically, and linguistically—of that region. It is important that literature from Africa be set in particular countries and portray the full range of venues, from rural to urban, traditional to modern, desert to jungle, poor to rich, historical to contemporary. Furthermore, readers can acquire misconceptions about literature from regions that may appear to be highly similar. We might assume, for example, that Canadians are very similar to Americans and that, therefore, their literature will be much like that from the United States, when in reality Canada has a rich, unique literary tradition. Pratt and Beaty (1999) note that this issue can particularly manifest itself in books written by outsiders to a country, who are generally less sensitive to how that region differs culturally from their own country. Cultural insiders, on the other hand, can be more attuned to subtle cultural nuances that are unapparent to non-natives.

Finally, even books that are culturally authentic can contribute to what is termed "essentializing"—assuming that all persons of the same culture share the same traits (Nodelman, 1996, p. 129). By this reasoning, when we read a book, such as Rahaman's *A Little Salmon for Witness: A Story from Trinidad* (1997) about a young boy who tries to find the perfect gift for his grandmother's birthday, we could assume that the character and lifestyle portrayed in the story exemplify the entire culture. This is a form of positive stereotyping and is just as problematic as negative stereotyping. When many books about a country are available, misconceptions, stereotypes, and questions of authenticity can be balanced (Pratt & Beaty, 1999). No single piece of literature or even a few works can give readers a well-rounded perspective of a culture, whereas diversity can counteract faulty perceptions and help readers ultimately gain their own sense of what is authentic.

Authenticity in Global Children's Literature

Authenticity often is associated with "insider-outsider" debates. The argument here is whether a writer (or illustrator) who is not a member of a culture can accurately present the perspective and experiences of characters from that group. Insider versus outsider perspective, however, begs the question: Who is a cultural insider and how can an insider's viewpoint be attained? Must an insider be a native of the country? What about emigrants and their children? How many generations removed from the country can descendants be and remain insiders? For example, can Ching Yeung Russell, who grew up in China but emigrated to the United States, accurately portray an experience in *Child Bride* (1999) that was not her own? Can a person who has lived in a country for a period of time be an insider? For example, Suzanne Fisher Staples was a journalist for many years in Asia, including Pakistan, where her novel, *Shabanu, Daughter of the Wind* (1989) is set, and she lived with nomads like Shabanu's family in the Cholistan Desert. What about a visitor who has traveled in a country extensively and done thorough research? For example, is Ted Lewin's 1995 visit to Morocco, where he "followed a storyteller through the cobbled streets" of Fez enough to qualify him (from New York) to write *The Storytellers* (1998)? Canadian Paul Morin provides more information in an author's note about how he traveled to northern Australia and met with Aboriginal storytellers to research his picture book, *Animal Dreaming: An Aboriginal Dreamtime Story* (1998). How can an insider's perspective be portrayed for groups of people who do not write about themselves, such as the Yanomami of the Amazon rain forest? After all, if only insiders can legitimately portray the perspective of a culture, the result may be *no* books about certain people and regions around the world.

Given the definition of international children's literature we have chosen for this book, these issues are real. We have decided to include not only books written and published first in countries other than the United States, but also books written by immigrants to the United States about their native countries and books written by American authors with settings in other countries. Thus, our definition may include books written by persons who are not true cultural insiders, a fact of which readers must be especially mindful as we consider global literature. Even more, authenticity is an issue when we evaluate literature for which we are cultural outsiders ourselves. How can we know what is culturally authentic? What if we lack basic information about the culture? How can or should we factor that knowledge or lack of knowledge into judgments about quality?

Different cultural norms influence the content and purposes of literature. In many countries, discussion of bodily functions and sexuality is more explicit and accepted than in the United States. How should readers and critics who are not from the country of the book react to such different norms? The clash of values between the culture of the book and the reader's culture may cause that reader to reject or react negatively to a literary work that may have nothing to do with the book's quality as literature. In addition, as discussed in Chapter 1, different countries can have very divergent purposes for children's literature. Some nations celebrate literature for its aesthetic value, while others view literature as primarily an educational tool with more pragmatic or even dogmatic intent. These differing purposes for literature lead to diverse standards for evaluating it: When emphasis is placed on literature's aesthetic qualities, literary standards will be applied and didacticism, specifically, is viewed negatively. On the other hand, educational purposes might permit or even favor didactic literature.

Even literary criteria, however, are not universal or culture-free. Traditional criteria used by critics in the United States to evaluate children's books derive largely from European and American aesthetic standards for literary elements (such as plot, theme, character, setting, and style) and literary structure (how those elements are combined into a literary work). Other cultures may not share the same standards or apply them in the same way. For example, some cultures may not place as much importance on plot as do Western Europeans and Americans. In pointing out the differences between Japanese and English writing styles, translator Cathy Hirano (1999) explains that "English is supposed to flow in a linear fashion, from introduction to body to conclusion . . . a book works toward a climax and then a conclusion. In contrast, Japanese composition appears almost circular" (p. 35). Even European and American cultures may value different types of plot structures. In Josef Holub's (1997) *The Robber and Me*, originally published in Germany, the plot may appear to meander at considerable length through seemingly disconnected scenes that are hard to distinguish as real or fantasy before finally beginning to reveal itself in a more straightforward manner well past the halfway point. Literary qualities, therefore, must be examined within the cultural context of the work, and admittedly, this is difficult for readers who are cultural outsiders!

Translation of International Children's Books

The Process of Translation

Translation can be defined as a linguistic science that conveys meaning from a source language to a target language. The process of translating any written text from one language into another is complex and challenging. When we consider translating a children's book from another language into English, additional challenges arise. Translators of children's books must consider their child audiences, the culture in which the book will be distributed, and the nuances of the different languages. As *Cricket Magazine* editor-in-chief, Marianne Carus (1980) has written, "Translators have a very delicate task: to interpret and to transfer the meaning from one language to another. Ideally they will be writers or creators, not just language experts" (p. 176). Oftentimes translators of children's books into English are further challenged because they may not be translating directly from the source language but from another translation of that language. For example, Rabinovici's 1999 Batchelder Award book, *Thanks to My Mother* (1998), originally written in Hebrew, was translated into English by James Skofield from the German translation.

Two of the most prominent translators of children's books into English are British translators Patricia Crampton and Anthea Bell. They have both translated books that have received the Batchelder Award: Anthea Bell translated the *Boys from St. Petri* by Reuter (1994) from Danish and *Konrad* by Nöstlinger (1977) from German; Patricia Crampton translated *No Hero for the Kaiser* by Frank (1986) from German and *Ronia, the Robber's Daughter* by Lindgren (1983) from Swedish. In addition, each has received the Astrid Lindgren Translation Prize awarded by the

Anthea Bell

Anthea Bell is one of the world's best-known translators of children's books into English. She translates books originally written in German, French, and Danish. Bell received both a bachelor's and master's degree from Oxford University and currently lives near Cambridge, England. Her career in children's book translating began in 1965 when she translated the German book *Robber Hotzenplotz* by Otfried Preussler into English. Since then, Bell has translated more than 200 books, including 29 titles in the French series "Asterix of Gaul" by Rene Goscinny.

Bell has received many honors for her work as a translator, including four Batchelder book awards: Reuter's *The Boys from St. Petri* (1994); Reuter's *Buster's World* (1989); Nöstlinger's *Konrad* (1977); and Hürlimann's *The Cat and Mouse Who Shared a House* (1974). In addition, she was honored with the Astrid Lindgren Prize for translation of works written for children, given by the International Federation of Translators, and the Schlegel-Tietk Prize for translation of German into English, an honor seldom accorded to children's books.

As noted in her biographical entry in *Something About the Author* (Hile, 1997), Bell believes that translated books both encourage children to learn other languages and enable ideas to be shared. Bell indicates that the translator's role "gives authors from other countries a voice as like their own as possible in which to address English-speaking children, so that their ideas can be passed on" (1997, p. 28).

In an interview with Ronald A. Jobe (1990), Bell notes the many challenges facing a children's book translator, one of which is "for a British translator to consider the importance of the American market" (p. 436) and the differences between British and American English. She explains that when an especially challenging dilemma occurs, she will consult someone in her international network of translators. For instance, some contemporary expressions and idioms may not be found in dictionaries and may be unknown to someone living in England.

As Jobe (1990) concludes, Bell uses "her talent, translation skills, and fluency with words for the betterment of the world we live in . . . What could be more beneficial than to provide English-speaking children with the opportunity to experience the best literature from other countries?" (p. 438).

International Federation of Translators—the only major award given to a children's book translator. In an interview with Ronald A. Jobe (1988), Crampton describes her commitment to providing children translated books: "Children are entitled to works of writers of genius. Children should not miss certain types of books not produced in our own language or country by our own English-speaking writers" (p. 411).

Every translator develops her or his own style and approach to the translation process. Anthea Bell, in an interview with Ronald Jobe (1990), describes that her goal is to produce "what the author might have written had he been writing in English in the first place" (p. 433). Bell reads the work before agreeing to translate it and then rereads it before beginning the translation process. She works on the computer and describes the importance of the word processor as allowing "her to print passages however many times are necessary for further revision" (Jobe,

p. 434). In a different approach, Patricia Crampton also reads the book prior to agreeing to translate it but then does not reread it again. Instead, she dictates the translation into a tape recorder, viewing translation as an "active performance" (Jobe, 1988, p. 412). After Crampton receives the transcribed copy of her recording, she begins the process of rewriting.

The qualities of a successful translator for children's books include fluency in both the source and target language, knowledge of both cultures, expertise in written language, and creativity. In addition, translators require "a knowledge of linguistics; an appreciation of literature for children; a writer's instincts; and an awareness of the interests of English-speaking children" (Jobe, 1996, p. 520). Translator Dagmar Hérrmann believes that "a translation succeeds only when children are astounded to find out that the book was originally published in another country, in another language" (Broderick, 1994, p. 40).

A translator of children's books faces many decisions that highlight some of the issues involved in translating from one language into another. The next section will discuss some of these issues.

Issues in Translation

In thinking about children's books in translation, one must constantly remember the tension between respect for the original text and respect for the intended audience of the work in translation. Klingberg (1986) identifies four goals for providing children translated books that influence how we might view this tension: increasing the amount of literature available to children; enhancing children's international perspective; providing children a text they can read and understand; and developing various values in children.

The complexities of translating children's books into English have led to many issues that translators have resolved in multiple ways, not always agreeing on the most appropriate resolution. First, the translator must decide if she or he will provide a literal translation of the work or attempt to convey the spirit of the work while considering the audience for the translated work: children living in a specific culture. Roger (1978) points out that "there is a responsibility of interpreting and translating the language so it remains faithful to the original text, yet has meaning for the reader. There is a voice of the translator that gives cohesion to the translation, an art form in itself, a voice that captures the sense and feeling of the original book smoothly, with no awareness that it is a translation" (p. 108). Because of differences in the source and target language, a literal translation may sound stilted and may be difficult for readers to understand, since many foreign words and phrases lack a precise English equivalent.

The translator must also determine the extent to which she or he will adapt the text to make the cultural context more meaningful to the target audience—that is, cultural context adaptation (Klingberg, 1986). This might involve changing the name of the main character or deleting a literary reference or references to mythology or popular beliefs that would be unknown to the target audience. Although many people believe that proper names should not be changed regardless of how difficult their pronunciation may be, others feel that changing names creates a more readable text for the intended audience. Then there is the question of how to handle references to historical, religious, and political background. Should all these be retained, and, if so, should something be done in the translation so these references are understood by readers in the target audience? Klingberg believes that various aspects of the foreign environment such as home furnishings, food, play, games, and customs ought to be retained and not deleted or changed in translation.

Nuances of language such as differences in grammar, writing style, language patterns, and vocabulary must be attended to by the translator. In addition, the translator should be sensitive to the level of reading difficulty for the intended audience. Word plays, idioms, and dialect are often challenging to translate into another language and still retain their meaning. Cathy Hirano (1999), who translated the Batchelder Award–winning novel *The Friends* by Yumoto (1996) from Japanese into English, discusses the ways Japanese differs from English in sentence structure. She notes that "Japanese sentences do begin with a subject, but it is often unstated and must be inferred from the context . . . The subject is followed by the object, and then finally the verb . . . The first task of a translator then is to unravel the sentence and rearrange the appropriate pieces in English order" (p. 35).

A controversial area is referred to by some as purification. This occurs when a perceived conflict in values exists between the source and target cultures. The translator then must decide if and how much to change the original text. For instance, as previously mentioned, European children's books generally reflect a more accepting attitude toward references to bodily functions and erotica than those originally published in the United States. An entire series of translated books from Japan on "My Body" includes such titles as Gomi's *Everyone Poops* (1993) and Cho's *The Gas We Pass: The Story of Farts* (1994). As noted in Chapter 1, realistic novels from Nordic countries are particularly known for their frank treatment of teenage sexuality. Moreover, many Holocaust novels and memoirs include detailed descriptions of persecution that may be considered too graphic and disturbing for American children.

Humorous elements of a book are often unique to a specific cultural context and may be expressed in specific ways linguistically. Hirano (1999) points out that a translator has a range of options in dealing with culturally specific humor from eliminating a joke completely to creating a new joke for the intended audience. She confronted this situation when translating a humorous incident in Yumoto's (1996) *The Friends* that she anticipated would not be funny to American audiences because of culturally specific references unknown to American children. Hirano consulted both her American editor and the Japanese author regarding a proposed solution. She notes, "The solution is a compromise: it does not convey the same meaning as the original Japanese, but at the same time it does not detract from the overall humor of the situation" (p. 41).

Finally, various genres present their own issues and challenges. For instance, nonfiction is generally considered easier to translate than fiction because it deals with factual material that usually has more readily accessible language equivalents. Poetry, on the other hand, is considered the most difficult because of the specific language patterns, rhythm, and rhyme characteristic of this genre. Some even believe that only poets should translate poetry (Carus, 1980). Then there is the dilemma of translating picture books because each word has been carefully selected to convey meaning and the text and illustrations work together to create a unified story. In many instances, styles of illustration may be appreciated differently so that criteria for what is considered a good illustration may be culturally specific. Tomlinson (1998) notes that taste in illustration may be culturally influenced and that "publishers have found that the stylistically sophisticated and symbol-rich picture books of some European artists . . . have not proven successful with young American audiences" (p. 19). Therefore, sometimes when text is translated the illustrations may be redone or altered by an American illustrator (Stan, 1999).

The process of translating a children's book from a source language into English is certainly not merely a linguistic science. Translation more closely resembles an art form in which the translator must recreate the story and language of an author so it can be enjoyed by children who speak and read a different language. Yet, a translation must remain true to the original author in tone, spirit and voice. The translator, through her or his own voice, must convey the unique aspects of the source culture while rendering a text that can be read and appreciated by American children.

Publishing and Distributing International Children's Books

How do international books come to be published and distributed in the United States? Many paths exist for an international book to reach children in the United States. As noted in Chapter 1, one way occurs at the Bologna Book Fair, held each Spring in Italy and attended by more than 1,200 publishers from around 80 countries. This fair is attended by publishers of children's and young adult books, literary agents, and children's book illustrators. At this fair, considered the major event for copyright business and international coproductions, publishers buy and sell rights to their books. Similarly, at BookExpo America, sponsored yearly by the American Booksellers Association, foreign book rights are negotiated. The American Booksellers Association is the trade association of the book publishing industry in the United States. The Biennale of Illustrations Bratislava (BIB), held every two years in this Slovak city, is an international juried competition for picture book illustrations. It first began in 1967, and today almost 300 illustrators representing 45 countries participate. Children's book publishers can also negotiate for rights to picture books there.

Another venue is through copublication agreements between a foreign publisher and a U.S. publisher. For instance, Rabén and Sjögren (R&S Books), the Swedish publisher, has such an agreement with Farrar, Straus, and Giroux so that books by Swedish authors are translated into English and distributed in the United States. R&S is responsible for the highly popular books about Linnea such as *Linnea in Monet's Garden* by Björk (1987). Several British companies have offices in the United States for distribution of their books, such as DK Publishing and Barefoot Books. Candlewick Press is the sister company of Walker Books Limited in the United Kingdom and Walker Books Australia. Edge Books, an imprint of Henry

Holt Books for Young Readers, specializes in multicultural and international books for young adults. Boyds Mills Press is distributing the picture books of Aile Cameroun, an organization of Cameroon authors and illustrators. Prominent children's book editors such as Margaret McElderry and the late Dorothy Briley have been influential in encouraging the publication of international children's books.

According to Jobe (1996), "The single most significant development in the international children's publishing industry has been the dramatic increase in the co-production of books" (p. 527). He points out that picture books are the most popular titles for co-production because "the art sells the book" (p. 527). Fiction titles are more problematic, since publishers must rely on individuals fluent in the original language of publication to read the book and report on its merits and marketability.

Generally, there is a lag of a few months to several years between original publication of a book and its translation and distribution in the United States. For example, Sortland's (1999) *Anna's Art Adventure* was originally published in Norway in 1993 and received many international honors including the IBBY Honour List Diploma before being translated and published in the United States by Carolrhoda Books in 1999. In commenting on this delay, an independent children's bookseller pointed out the impact that the Internet may have on U.S. publishing of international children's books. She cited the example of the popular Harry Potter books and how American buyers were logging on to Amazon.UK to order the books before titles were even available in England, let alone the United States. This caused Scholastic Publishing, which owns the U.S. rights to Harry Potter, to move up its publication dates for each of the books (Sally Oddi, personal communication, August 1999).

Several United States publishing companies specialize in translated books of which Kane/Miller Book Publishers and North-South Books are two examples. North-South Books is the English-language imprint of the Swiss publisher Nord-Süd Verlag. In addition to distributing English-language editions of the Swiss books, it also publishes original children's books. North-South is probably best known for bringing U.S. children the Rainbow Fish books by Marcus Pfister. Kane/Miller is an independent book company that specializes in foreign children's books. As stated in its catalogue, Kane/Miller's goals are "open-minded books opening young minds to the world" and "bringing the world closer to a child and the children of the world closer to each other."

In 1998 about 3,400 new children's books were published in the United States. Of these, only 22, less than 1% were imported titles (Bogart, 1999). However, this number is somewhat misleading since co-productions and books published by international companies with offices in the United States are not considered. This very low percentage is consistent, however, with data presented by Tomlinson (1998) that indicate that the percentage of translated/imported books ranged from less than 1% to 1.7% between 1991 and 1995. Stan (1999) estimates that international books comprise 5% of children's books published each year in the United States. She indicates that "between 1 and 2 percent are translations; the remaining books having been first published in the English language in Great Britain, Australia, Canada, New Zealand, or South Africa" (p. 174). Although statistics were not available specifically for children's literature, information about all books translated into English and published in the United States in 1998 indicated that over half of the total imported books had been translated from French or German (Bogart, 1999). White (1992), in a study on translated books, found that of the more than 58,000 children's books in print in 1990, only 572 were translated. Of these, the majority were translated from German, French, Swedish, and Danish.

In an interview, Sally Oddi, owner of an independent bookstore, Cover-to-Cover Books in Columbus, Ohio, offered her perspective as a children's bookseller regarding the international children's book market. Oddi provided insight into how she selects books to stock in her store and indicated her desire "to read the book myself and make my own decision how it will sell in my market. Just because it is a hit in England does not necessarily mean it will be a hit here" (Oddi, personal communication, August 1999). She also pointed out some differences in interest in terms of age range. For instance, many of the European novels for middle readers are more complex in content, sophisticated in theme, and franker in language dealing with sensitive topics than their U.S. counterparts. Oddi may market these exclusively for young adult readers rather than for both an upper elementary and young-adult market. She noted that some international titles sell very well, such as *Linnea in Monet's Garden,* while others may sell only a few copies.

Many impediments exist to the distribution of international books in the United States. Certainly the added costs of securing the rights, paying for a translation, and selecting a translator when there exists a shortage of highly qualified translators are problems. Because editors may not be fluent in the original language of the book, they may not be able to determine the quality of the translation. Publishers must consider the marketability of a book and whether the costs of obtaining the foreign rights and paying for translation will be compensated for by sales. In addition, many individuals convey the attitude that the United States has more than enough of its own children's books and that importing titles is not necessary to meet the reading needs of American children.

In her study of successful translated children's books, White (1992) looked for patterns among books that remained in print longer than four years and had received a favorable review or an award in the United States. Of the 131 books in her sample, she found that fantasy, folklore, and fiction were the most frequently represented genres and that poetry and biography were least represented. Although not included separately in her genre categories, 34 books were picture books and 25 were identified as classics. The major subject areas reflect those with universal appeal such as folklore, animal stories, and novels focusing on children's lives. She concluded that "publishers continue primarily to publish children's classics, books from the public domain, and the works of popular authors" (p. 270).

Selecting and Evaluating Global Children's Literature

All these issues have important implications for selecting and evaluating global children's literature. One important consideration concerns how cultural outsiders can evaluate books from or about other countries. How can we know what is culturally authentic when we are not a part of those cultures or when we lack even basic knowledge about a culture? Rudine Sims Bishop's (1992) advice for selecting multicultural literature holds equally true for global literature: Become informed about the literature. First, this involves learning about the various types of multicultural (and global) literature, of which she identifies three categories. *Culturally specific* books characterize a particular, identifiable culture. For example, Frances Temple's gripping novel *Tonight, by Sea* (1995) could take place only in Haiti in 1993. Not only is the story rich with cultural details, but the plot revolves around the oppression that many poor people experienced at that time in Haiti and their determination to seek freedom. *Culturally generic* books portray characters of a cultural group but contain few details specific to that culture. *Halinka* (1998), by Mirjam Pressler, is a novel set in post–World War II Germany about a girl who lives in a home for emotionally disturbed girls, but while the setting serves as a backdrop for this story, specific cultural information is very limited. It could almost take place anywhere. *Culturally neutral* books feature characters of a cultural group "but are fundamentally about something else" (p. 46). Eric Campbell's *Papa Tembo* (1998) is a contemporary novel set in East Africa about the reality of elephant poaching and both the involvement and resistance by some tribal groups. However, the story's main focus is on the plight of the elephants, rather than the impact of the elephant trade on the lives of indigenous people.

In addition to awareness about the types of literature, Bishop (1992) advocates extensive reading of literature written by cultural insiders. Doing this acquaints readers with the "themes, topics, values, attitudes, language features, [and] social mores" (p. 46) that typify the literature of a culture and helps readers gain a sense of the characteristics of the group's literature. This insight can be used as a benchmark against which to judge other literature about the featured culture. However, as noted earlier, the availability of global children's literature will influence readers' opportunity for wide reading about specific cultures. Ensuring both knowledgeable readers and high literary quality begins with access to as much diverse literature as possible.

Given certain cautions—the cultural contextuality of literary standards and the issues associated with literature written and evaluated by cultural outsiders—we propose the following criteria for selecting and evaluating global children's literature.

Literary Merit

Educators and scholars in the United States operate within the context of generally recognized literary criteria against which to judge all literature, including global children's literature. According to many experts (e.g., Bishop, 1992; Cullinan & Galda, 1998; Lynch-Brown & Tomlinson, 1999; Temple, Martinez, Yokota, & Naylor, 1998), culturally diverse literature must first qualify as good literature. Huck, Hepler, Hickman, and Kiefer (1997) identify the following guidelines for evaluating fiction: (1) a plot that is original, fresh, well-constructed, and credible; (2) a setting that contributes to a story's mood and authenticity; (3) worthwhile themes that emerge naturally and subtly from the narrative; (4) characters who are convincing, consistent, and well-developed; (5) a style that is suited to the plot, theme, characters, and tone of the story; and (6) a clearly identifiable point of view that offers readers insight about their lives and world. Overall, there also is the consideration of how each and all of these elements work together to create a coherent, unified whole.

As an example of applying these criteria to a work of fiction, we analyze Susan Fletcher's *Shadow Spinner* (1998). Here is a plot in the classic romance form (Sloan, 1991) with a dash of mystery thrown in. In fact, this novel is based upon the Shahrazad legend from the 1,001 Arabian Nights tales and is set in ancient Persia, thought by many scholars to be the true source for the stories, according to Fletcher's author's note. Thus, its structure is that of folklore and involves wish-fulfillment and a quest for the story that Shahrazad needs to continue to live. Shahryar, the sultan, had been taking a new wife every day and having her killed after one night to avoid the pain he experienced when his first wife was unfaithful to him. Every young woman and girl in the kingdom is at risk until Shahrazad bravely volunteers to become his wife in an effort to stop the killings. For more than 2 years, Shahrazad is able to pacify Shahryar by telling him stories each night that bring her a reprieve so that she can tell him more the next night. Marjan, a slave girl from whose point of view the story is told, is brought to Shahrazad's attention, when Marjan is heard telling a story to the palace harem's children and Shahrazad has run out of new stories to tell Shahryar after 989 nights. The story Marjan tells Shahrazad turns out to be one of Shahryar's favorites from his childhood, and he wishes to hear the sequel that he only faintly recollects. When Shahrazad summons Marjan again, the girl is terrified because she does not know the sequel, having heard only the first part from a blind storyteller in the bazaar. Thus begins the dangerous quest to find the storyteller and obtain the rest of the story in order to save Shahrazad's and all other young women's lives. Intrigue ensues with the mystery of who the "blind" storyteller really is and the suspense of whether the evil Khatun (Shahryar's mother), who is jealously protective of her son and wishes to dispose of Shahrazad, will be able to prevent Marjan from being successful. This plot line will keep young readers engrossed to the satisfying outcome—one that is somewhat predictable, as befits this type of story.

Fletcher brings the setting to life through her use of richly descriptive language to evoke detailed images of the sights, sounds, and smells of the Sultan's harem, the fabulous palace, the baths, the huge bazaar, and the poverty of the storyteller's neighborhood. Atmosphere hazy with dust, smoke, or steam, smells of incense and perfume, and sounds of splashing fountains and tinkling harem bells all contribute to the legendary, exotic mood suitable for this story. The twin characters of Marjan and Shahrazad can be taken as two sides of the same person: one poor, uneducated, crippled, and clumsy, and the other the embodiment of wealth, beauty, grace, privilege, and learning. However, unlike the usual Cinderella rags-to-riches transformations, both of these characters are clever, gifted storytellers ("shadow spinners"), and each one needs the other to be complete. Shahrazad needs Marjan's street savvy and Marjan needs Shahrazad's knowledge of palace intrigue to make the quest a success. Shahrazad helps Marjan to reconcile her anger toward her mother, who deliberately crippled Marjan as a young child to protect her from the Sultan and then committed suicide. Marjan saves Shahrazad's life, not only with the specific story Shahryar requests, but also with one of her own creation that helps him finally to trust Shahrazad and end the death threat. Other characters serve fairly typical one-dimensional folk tale roles: the fairy god-mother–like Zaynab, the pigeon keeper; the wicked witch–like Khatun; and the helpful, mysterious storyteller.

Throughout the narrative runs the symbolism of stories and storytelling, building the theme of life reflecting stories and stories influencing life. Stories, as life, often probe the nature of love and forgiveness, a theme that both Marjan and Shahryar must confront, and do so in a manner that is more acceptable to the listener than direct advice. Furthermore, the ability to tell stories and to use language is a means for the weak and downtrodden to gain power, which links to another theme that explores issues of gender and class equality, justice for the oppressed, and the triumph of good over evil—ideas that are simultaneously ancient and contemporary. The novel's structure is strengthened with the "Lessons for Life and Storytelling" that begin each chapter—pithy commentaries that foreshadow events in the chapter and tightly unify the individual elements of the story into a coherent, satisfying whole. This novel, then, as judged by established literary criteria, well meets the qualities of good literature and should resonate with the interests of upper elementary to middle school children, who will enjoy the exciting, adventuresome plot, identify with the memorable characters, and understand the worthwhile, relevant themes.

In addition to fiction, other genres—folklore, poetry, and information books—have their own criteria for excellence. Cullinan and Galda (1998) state that folklore should: "retain the flavor of the oral form; have natural, easily spoken rhythms; reflect the integrity of early retellings; avoid controlled, diluted, or trite vocabulary"; and have illustrations that "complement and extend the narrative, portray the traditional character of the tale, and reflect the cultural heritage of the tale" (p. 166). Poetry should be understandable for children, stir their emotions, create sensory images, have language that plays with sounds and/or echoes the meaning, match rhythm with meaning, and have a form appropriate for the content. Among the criteria for nonfiction are these important considerations: distinguishing fact from theory; acknowledging different points of view; supporting generalizations with facts; providing documentation; identifying the author's qualifications and/or consultants; writing in an appropriate, engaging, understandable style; being well-organized, clear, and supported with such features as a table of contents, index, or bibliography; having an attractive layout and design; and using illustrations or graphics to support the information.

Thus, while recognizing the potential cultural bias of these criteria, we do evaluate global works against the same standards used to judge all literature. At the same time, we need to educate ourselves about the literary values of other cultures around the world and add those to our critical repertoires. One way to do this is by studying books that have won literary awards in their own countries, such as Tim Wynne-Jones's *Some of the Kinder Planets* (1995), which won the Canadian Governor General's Literary Award in 1993, or Yumoto's *The Friends* (1996), which won the Recommended Book Prize from Japan School Library Book Club. Other award winners in their respective countries that are discussed in Chapter 4 include *92 Queens Way* by Case (1995), *Flour Babies* by Fine (1994), and *I Miss You, I Miss You!* by Pohl and Gieth (1999).

Author's Background, Qualifications, and Point of View

One of the first things that readers can do when encountering a new book is to examine the dust jacket or any additional inside information provided about the author. How much of a cultural insider does the author appear to be? What knowledge or experiences does the author have that qualify him or her to write a story set in a particular country? For example, where does the author currently live and where was he or she born? What other books, if any, has the author written and what do you know about their authenticity? Furthermore, as you read the book, what can you tell about the author's perspective on and attitudes about the culture represented in the story? Is the author able to write a story that offers the intimacy of an insider's perspective? Does the author seem like a credible informant about the culture represented? Is the point of view of the narrative appropriate for the author's background and qualifications?

Abelove's *Go and Come Back* (1998) is a particularly interesting case in point. This contemporary novel is set in a Peruvian jungle village where two "old white ladies" from New York have just arrived. They are anthropologists (actually in their 20s) who live with and study the Isabos for one year. Although Joanna and Margarita try to gain acceptance by the villagers, their own values differ sharply from those of the Isabo in such areas as sex, ownership and stinginess, lying, and partying. In spite of these differences, however, they do forge a friendship with Alicia, a girl on the brink of womanhood. She finds them puzzling, but she also is intrigued by them and shows them the ways of her people. In essence, she watches them as much as they study her and the villagers. One could say that the author, an anthropologist who lived in the Amazon jungle for two years with people much like these, would be eminently qualified to write such a story. Complicating that fact, though, is the narrative's point of view—that of Alicia. The result is a story that turns ethnographic research and the clash of cultures upside down, as we view the anthropologists' well-meaning endeavors from a cultural insider's perspective. Thus, one of the themes of this intriguing story is the question of cultural authenticity, as the narrative becomes a kind of metafiction about insider-outsider perspective.

Portrayal of Characters

Readers also should examine books to identify any character stereotypes. (In fact, as noted earlier, popular stereotypes prevalent in the United States about particular cultures, may determine what global literature is even available for readers.) From what you know about the story's culture, are the characters portrayed appropriately? Are they realistic as human beings, with both evident strengths and weaknesses? Are the characters within the story as diverse as you would expect in your own culture? How do characters achieve success? For example, do they have to give up their own cultural distinctiveness and adopt that of another more powerful culture in order to achieve their goals (Nodelman, 1996)?

In Uri Orlev's historical novel, *Lydia, Queen of Palestine* (1993), readers encounter a rich palate of character types. Lydia is a memorable, strong-willed, and far-from-perfect character. Her mother, jealous and angry about her father's infidelity, leaves Lydia home alone much of the time (since Lydia cannot behave with nannies) when Lydia is still quite young—hardly the image of an ideal parent. Still, her mother sacrifices her chance for freedom to ensure Lydia's escape from Nazi-controlled Romania. Later, at the kibbutz in Palestine, Lydia meets individuals who treat her both well and poorly. Finally, when she is reunited with her father and his new wife, Lydia gains some surprising insights about two persons she had believed were completely evil. The realistic characters and their relationships make this story highly believable.

Another aspect of characterization that is important to investigate is the way relationships between characters from different cultures are portrayed in the story. What are the power relationships in the narrative and how are they treated? Who takes leadership and resolves the problems in the story? For example, in *The Shaman's Apprentice: A Tale of the Amazon Rain Forest* (1998) by Lynne Cherry and Mark J. Plotkin, the Tirio Indians in the Amazon rain forest had always followed the traditional healing practices of their shaman, until malaria is introduced to their village by outsider gold seekers. White missionaries then provide them with quinine pills, which cure the malaria but also cause the villagers to no longer trust their shaman's medicine. Eventually, another outsider (who may be Hispanic) reconfirms the shaman's knowledge and restores the villagers' respect for his powers. Astute readers will be wary of character relationships that reflect traditional cultural dominance such as this.

Language

As Bishop (1992) explained, literature written by cultural insiders is more likely to contain language patterns that are authentic. Without being from the country depicted in the story, readers will need to judge how credible is the language used by characters in the story and even the loyalty of the narrator's voice to the culture. Does the language ring true, or does it seem as if a cultural outsider is trying to sound like a native? In particular, it is important to be sensitive to any potentially offensive terms. If such terms are used, what is their purpose and importance?

For example, Amy Browen Zemser, who lived in Liberia for three years, depicts the Liberian dialect in her contemporary novel, *Beyond the Mango Tree* (1998). In this story about a friendship that develops between an American girl and a Liberian boy, Boima's dialect is captured when he tells Sarina what he can offer her: "I can take you to see different-different thing. Me part, I know Monrovia too good-o. I can show you the cityside an' the sea. I know from Duport Road to the Bong Mine Bridge. Liberia all right-o" (p. 32). Given the author's extensive experiences in the country, the dialect seems credible and appropriate. In fact, the language gives readers a strong sense of the local culture, and it is used respectfully.

Illustrations

In picture books, the illustrations contribute substantially to the development of characterization and setting, and to a lesser degree to plot, themes, style, and point of view. The same attributes that are important for evaluating characterization in text are valid for illustrations. It is essential that pictures show diversity and avoid stereotypes with respect to characters. For example, are facial features varied to the same degree that they would be in the cultural environment? Jesse Sweetwater researched her acrylic, watercolor, and gouache illustrations for *Bouki Dances the Kokioko: A Comical Tale from Haiti* by Wolkstein (1997) through Haitian history, culture, and art. The human features in this story are exaggerated and possibly for that reason could be considered stereotypical. However, they also are varied—long and wide noses, full and thin lips, round and sunken cheeks, slanted and round eyes. Skin tones range from caramel to dark chocolate, and body shapes show equal differences.

In addition, illustrations can establish the setting in picture books that otherwise do not develop the setting through the text. Illustrators always need to do meticulous research to portray the setting of the story accurately, which is especially important for books set in other countries. Here the illustrations must carry much of the cultural information for readers. When Sharon Wilson from Bermuda created her pastel illustrations for *The Day Gogo Went to Vote: South Africa April 1994* (1996), by Elinor Batezet Sisulu from South Africa, she traveled to the country and spoke with and photographed people there. Because of this research, images of the township in the story are realistic enough to show chickens roaming freely around the houses and nuclear plant towers in the background.

Translation

Because we most likely will not possess the language proficiency to compare the translated work with the original, it is difficult to determine the accuracy and effectiveness of the translation itself. However, there are a few criteria to consider when selecting a translated work in addition to the general criteria discussed in this chapter. First, it is important to note if the translator has been acknowledged. Does his or her name appear in the book or is there merely a general reference to translation by the publisher? Oftentimes personal information about the translator is included on the book jacket with information about the author. In that way, readers can assess at least minimally the background and qualifications of the translator.

A second criterion to consider is whether the book has received any awards either in the country of origin, within the international literary community, or in the United States. These awards are sometimes designated by seals on the book jacket or information somewhere in the book or on the jacket highlighting the award. In addition, sometimes there may be a note from the publisher, author, or translator providing additional information about the book and the translation.

For example, we can apply these criteria to Holub's 1998 Batchelder Award winning novel, *The Robber and Me* (1997). The information "Translated from the German by Elizabeth D. Crawford" appears on the title page. On the book jacket flap, there are two short biographies, one about the author Josef Holub and one about the translator. We learn that books by Elizabeth Crawford were previously honored by the Batchelder committee. In a "Translator's Note" at the end of the book, Crawford provides additional information about German history and geography for readers and gives insight into the spelling of German words. Thus, this book meets the criteria for excellence in translation.

In addition, the International Relations Committee of the Association for Library Service to Children (1998) discusses the criteria used by the Batchelder Award committee in selecting translated books for that award. These criteria include:

> Tell a good story . . . ; be smoothly translated and, at the same time, true to the country and culture of origin; not be unduly Americanized; possess literary elements . . . ; provide illustrations, type, layout, and jacket design that enhance the text and do not detract from it; include information that is accurate, clear, and well organized; and appeal to children. (p. 264–265)

Accuracy

Overall, accuracy is critical to every aspect of a global book. Here, readers should not only be alert to inaccuracies, but should also be aware that significant omissions are cause for concern. An example of an apparent inaccuracy appears in *The Distant Talking Drum* (1995), Isaac Olaleye's collection of poetry from Nigeria. Frané Lessac, from Australia, created the shimmering gouache illustrations for this book, as she has done so beautifully for several other books set in the Caribbean. Her naive style portrays the charm of village life in a tropical rain forest, but, in one illustration, what looks like a tiger is strutting on the roof of a house. However, there are no native tigers in Africa, only lions, leopards, and cheetahs.

It is always helpful when authors and illustrators who are cultural outsiders to some degree provide information in the book about the extent of their experiences in the culture, the research they have conducted, or the experts they have consulted to verify the accuracy of their work. When such information is given, readers can feel more confident about the book's trustworthiness, but when little or no information appears, readers who are cultural outsiders face a more difficult task.

Reader's Point of View

Finally, there are two considerations regarding the reader's perspective. First, as cultural outsiders to a particular country portrayed in a book, we can consult with persons who have more expertise about that country or who are even cultural insiders. What is their opinion of the book? Do they discover problems that we overlook, assumptions that we take for granted? From what basis do their views stem? How trustworthy are their perceptions? What qualifies them as experts or insiders? How do they compare to one's own or others' judgments? Some of these "expert" or "insider" evaluations may be available to readers through professional reviews, and we need to consult such sources as widely as possible. Secondly, readers should be mindful of how we would feel if the book we are considering were written about our country or culture. If the story's depictions would offend us, they might well be unacceptable to natives of another country.

As examples of the reader's perspective, we draw upon those of the two authors of this book. When Evelyn Freeman, who is Jewish, reads a picture book such as Barbara Smucker's *Selina and the Shoo-fly Pie* (1998), about a nineteenth-century Mennonite girl living in Canada, she can call upon the relative insider's perspective of Barbara Lehman, who is Mennonite, to verify the authenticity of this book in both text and illustration. Likewise, when Barbara reads a book such as the historical novel *Under the Domim Tree* by Israeli author Gila Almagor (1995), about three girls living in an Israeli youth village in 1953, she can discuss with Evelyn Freeman, who has visited Israel on three separate occasions, the authenticity of the text's characters and setting.

Conclusion

The issues presented in this chapter are complex and not easily resolved. However, awareness of them is an important first step, and there are additional measures to pursue. We can make every effort to find and read as much literature about as many countries, across as many genres, and depicting as much variety within countries as possible, remembering that no one book portrays everything about a single culture. As cultural outsiders, we can be sensitive to the issue of authenticity and critically examine a book's authorship and the cultural context from which a book emerges. When we understand the constraints of translation, we can look for works that seem true to the original while being accessible to an audience from another country (and keep an open mind about cultural values that may differ from our own!). We need to recognize and support the efforts of publishers who bring international books to the U.S. market and learn about the literature of other countries and cultures so that we become less culturally biased in how we apply literary criteria to various genres. In particular, we should carefully examine the author's point of view, the book's portrayal of characters, and its language, illustrations, and accuracy. Finally, we need to consult readers (personally or through written reviews) who may enlighten us with an insider's perspective.

Crossing international boundaries through literature propels us out of our comfort zone, but it is an exciting and rewarding adventure. Such issues as availability, authenticity, translation, and publication are daunting enough, but selection and evaluation of global literature may seem overwhelming when we are not familiar with the countries and cultures depicted. There are so many points to consider, and our knowledge base may seem hopelessly small. However, the important thing, we believe, is to keep an open mind, be sensitive and ready to revise our understanding, and continue to learn as much as possible about the whole world of children's literature. To that end, the next chapter will examine six genres of global literature in more depth.

4 Trends in Global Children's Literature: Focus on Genre

"You should be taught peace, understanding, tolerance, and friendship among all people." This tenth principle of the Convention of the Rights of the Child adopted by the United Nations General Assembly in 1989 is certainly being supported and promoted through international children's literature. Children around the world can learn the meaning of these principles as they read contemporary children's literature. In this chapter we describe some current trends in global children's literature and organize this discussion around six major genres: picture books, fiction, informational books, biography/autobiography and memoir, poetry, and folklore. We use genres as our framework because we believe that an understanding of global literature should be grounded in knowledge of the history, characteristics, and values of these categories. We further organize our analysis of the books within each genre by themes, content, or other traits that we believe teachers will find useful in their work with children. Because this book's scope is limited to children's books available in the United States, the coverage of current trends does not represent the vast array of children's books worldwide that are inaccessible to American audiences. We have tried, in the discussion of each genre, to highlight a small sample of titles that represent the trends discussed. Other recent titles that also contribute to these trends are referenced in other chapters of this book.

Picture Books

Picture books, with their combination of the verbal and visual, speak "two languages" by their very nature. These two modes, working together, offer unique opportunities to experience other cultures that books with text alone cannot provide. Words and pictures, according to Nodelman (1988), "both define and amplify each other" (p. viii) and must allow room for each to do its work of telling a story. Thus, where text may include unfamiliar words or concepts, illustrations can clarify or show. Likewise, where pictures may portray unfamiliar environments, words can explain.

The earliest children's picture books with identified illustrators mostly originated in England. The art of Walter Crane, Randolph Caldecott (for whom the U.S. medal for illustration is named), Kate Greenaway (namesake for the British medal for illustration), Leslie Brooke, Beatrix Potter, and Arthur Rackham has been well-known in the United States since the late nineteenth and early twentieth centuries and for many years "supplied the American picture book market" (Huck, Hepler, Hickman, & Kiefer, 1997, p. 104). Since then, several non-British Hans Christian Andersen award winners have become especially familiar to American audiences, including Mitsumasa Anno (from Japan), Lizbeth Zwerger (from Austria), and Tomi Ungerer (from France). The work of Italian artist Bruno Munari, Australians Julie Vivas and Jan Ormerod, South African Niki Daly, and Swiss Felix Hoffmann and Marcus Pfister also has been widely available in the U.S. market, along with that of more recent British illustrators, such as John Burningham, Shirley Hughes, Pat Hutchins, Raymond Briggs, Janet Ahlberg, Michael Foreman, and Anthony Browne. Several picture books have been recognized with the Mildred Batchelder Award for translated books, particularly Toshi Maruki's (1982) *Hiroshima No Pika* and *Rose Blanche* by Christophe Gallaz and Roberto Innocenti (1985), both accounts of the horrors of World War II. In addition, there are now many Americans who illustrate stories about other cultures around the world.

In this section, we will explore three aspects of recent trends in selected global picture books: thematic or topical content, illustration styles, and cultural information available through illustrations. We also note how modern picture book creation can bring together authors and illustrators from different countries.

Content

The kinds of stories with international connections reveal a distinct contrast between fantasy (particularly animal) and realism. Of the recent animal (or creature) fantasy books, most were originally published abroad with non-American authors/illustrators. According to Stan (1999), animal fantasies more easily make the transition to an American market because geographical settings are "not a strongly defined element of the story" (p. 175), thus allowing them to be more "universal." For example, Marcus Pfister's highly popular *The Rainbow Fish* (1992) and his more recent *Milo and the Magical Stones* (1997), both originally published by Nord-Süd Verlag AG in Switzerland, are two premier examples of this trend. In the latter book, Pfister continues his trademark style of glittery overlays embedded in the pictures—in this case, the magical stones that Milo, the mouse, discovers one day. At the point when Milo must make an ethical decision about how to share the stones with the other mice, the format of the book splits in half to show the rest of the story moving toward two endings, one happy and one sad.

Swede Lars Klinting has written and illustrated *Bruno the Carpenter* (1996a), originally published by Alfabeta Bokförlag AB, about a beaver who decides to build a toolbox to organize his messy workshop. The book includes labeled pictures of all Bruno's tools and plans for the toolbox construction. Endpapers are simulated wood. Another book about the busy beaver, *Bruno the Tailor* (1996b), recounts his efforts to sew an apron and includes similar features.

Henry & Horace Clean Up (1996), by German author Wolfgang Mennel and German illustrator Gisela Dürr, was first published by Michael Neugebauer Verlag AG in Switzerland. This charming story describes an elephant (Horace) and a pig (Henry) who are friends, but opposites in their housekeeping habits. Horace keeps his house in perfect order, while Henry's house is, well, a pigsty. Henry cajoles Horace into moving all of his disarray into Horace's home, with disastrous results. Henry makes amends for his scam by promising to fix everything the next day and sharing his treasure of books with Horace in the meantime around a campfire that night.

French author-illustrator Gilles Eduar takes readers on a *Dream Journey* (1999) in a story first published in France by Albin Michel Jeunesse. Anatole the camel takes the boy Jules on a fantasy trip around the world to unique experiences and "places rarely seen": mermaids in the Southern Sea, the jungle east of Quito, a bicycle ride through busy streets, a climb up the highest mountain peak, and a slide down a snowy hillside. Interestingly, the gouache and acrylic paintings are on newspaper classified advertisements that show through the paint in places and appear to be written in English.

Russian Nikolai Popov's (1996) wordless fable *Why?* originally was published by Michael Neugebauer Verlag AG in Switzerland. This graphic tale depicts the beginning of a fight between a frog and a mouse who steals the frog's flower. From that point, an arms race escalates until the landscape is blackened and all life is destroyed, except for the frog and mouse. An author's note explains Popov's boyhood experiences that provided the impetus for the story's theme of the devastation of war and consequences of violence.

Finally, well-known Australian author Mem Fox and Australian illustrator Kerry Argent collaborated on *Wombat Divine* (1996), which Omnibus Books first published in 1995 in Australia. In this gentle story, Wombat wants most of all to earn a part in the Nativity play, but it seems that he is unsuitable for any of the roles for which he auditions. He is too heavy to be the Archangel Gabriel, too big to be Mary, too short to be a king, and so on. Finally, after all the parts are seemingly distributed, Bilby suggests that Wombat would be perfect for the Baby Jesus. Fox continues her tradition of introducing readers to animals of her native land—such as the wombat, bilby, emu, numbat, and kangaroo—as she did in her earlier *Koala Lou* (1989) and *Possum Magic* (1990). Thus American readers have the opportunity to learn about Australia, as well as be entertained.

On the other hand, books with international connections written and illustrated by Americans (even recent immigrants) are predominately realistic stories published in the United States. For example, Nigerian-born immigrant Isaac Olaleye recounts the adventure of two boys, Ade and Tayo, in *Lake of the Big Snake* (1998). The pair disobey their mothers' warning not to leave the village while the two women go to visit another village. Of course, Ade and Tayo go into the jungle to play and end up at the lake, where a large water snake terrifies them. After several mishaps, the two escape and return home to face the consequences with their mothers. Claudia Shepard's watercolor illustrations capture the setting and boys' antics well.

Cristina Kessler's (1995b) *One Night: A Story from the Desert* portrays the life of Tuaregs she met when she was a Peace Corps volunteer in Niger. Muhamad leads his

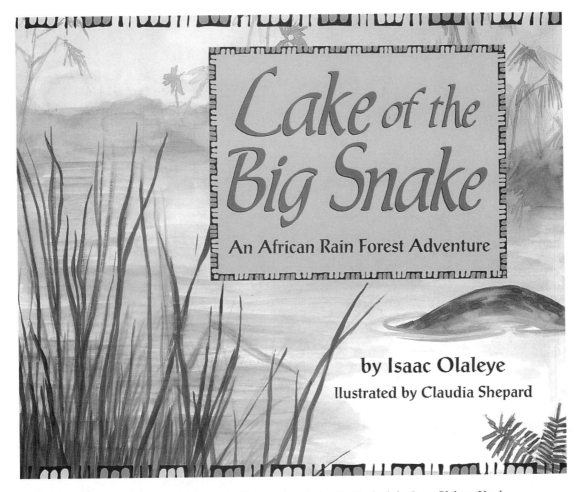

Jacket illustration copyright © 1998 by Claudia Shepard from *Lake of the Big Snake* by Isaac Olaleye. Used with permission of Boyds Mills Press.

goat herd to graze each day, fulfilling an important role for his family. One evening as he returns home with the herd, a mother goat goes into labor, and Muhamad realizes that he and the rest of the herd will have to spend the night alone. The kid's safe delivery tests his skills and earns him a place among the men. Ian Schoenherr's double-spread impressionistic paintings evoke the desert's rich colors and vastness and the narrative's theme of a way of life that shows respect for nature.

A third story from Africa, *Ndito Runs* by Laurie Halse Anderson (1996), tells the simple experience of rural Kenyan children who run miles to school each day. A young girl, Ndito, imagines many native animals to keep her company on her race: gazelles, goats, dik-diks, wildebeests, cranes, ostriches, and flamingos. She even passes her brothers, who had left her behind earlier. South African artist Anita van der Merwe used bold, earth-toned acrylics to embody this story's energy and carefree joy.

Amelia Lau Carling, now an American resident, drew upon her childhood as a daughter of Chinese immigrants to Guatemala in *Mama & Papa Have a Store* (1998). The book describes a day in their store, their customers (Spanish, Indian, and Chinese), what happens on the street outside, the noontime meal in their home behind the store, playing on the roof terrace, and evening chores. This slice of daily life, conveyed in text that includes Spanish words and bright, detailed watercolor and gouache paintings, shows the rich intermingling of three cultures.

Vashanti Rahaman, born in Trinidad and now living in the United States, used her childhood memories to create *O Christmas Tree* (1996). Anslem hopes their family will get a real Christmas tree this year—a tree that must travel a long distance from its native northern environment to reach his warm climate. By the time these trees reach his island, they are only dry brush, not the fresh, green-needled variety he imagined. When Anslem tries to make do by painting two of the dead trees white, he ends up with a mess and no tree. Finally, his neighbor helps him recognize the abundant native Christmas trees—poinsettias. Lilting dialect and Australian Frané Lessac's festive, naive gouache illustrations bring to life a Caribbean culture.

Saturday Sancocho and its Spanish edition, *El sancocho del sábado*, is Colombian-born (now U.S. resident) Leyla Torres's (1995) delightful story of Maria Lili's Saturday tradition of making sancocho with her grandparents. One Saturday, there are only eggs available and no money to buy the ingredients for the special stew. Undaunted, Mama Ana uses the eggs to barter in the market for plantains, cassava, corn, carrots, onions, tomatoes, cilantro, garlic, cumin, and a chicken—all the necessary items for delicious sancocho. (A recipe for the stew is included at the end of the book.) The author's soft watercolor, double-spread illustrations realistically portray the home and village market settings.

Finally, *Mei-Mei Loves the Morning,* by American Margaret Holloway Tsubakiyama (1999), depicts another close relationship between a child and her grandfather. Mei-Mei and her grandfather awaken before the rest of the family, eat breakfast together, and set off with their caged songbird on Grandpa's bicycle for the park. Readers experience the sights of busy city streets, the round moon gate, and activities in the park: tai-chi exercises, drinking tea, and conversing with friends. Finally, on their way home, they stop for pancakes from a street vendor. Cornelius Van Wright and Ying-Hwa Hu created the double-spread illustrations with watercolors and pencils to complement this glimpse of contemporary Chinese life.

Illustration Styles

Across global picture books, we find a wide range of artistic styles represented. These reflect many of the common styles found in the art world in general, such as representational, impressionism, expressionism, naive, and cartoon art. For example, in many of the realistic stories already described, the illustrations also are realistic or representational. According to Cianciolo (1997), this style "offers direct observations of the reality [the artist] has observed or experienced" (p. 28). Caroline

Binch's illustrations for British author Mary Hoffman's (1995) *Grace & Family* (sequel to *Amazing Grace* [1991]) offer another example of representational art. Here, realistic watercolor paintings accompany the story of Grace's trip with her Nana from England to The Gambia to visit her father and his new family. Details of their home, the market, Gambian clothing, and activities—such as eating benachim, dancing, and petting tame crocodiles—are faithfully depicted.

In *Jamela's Dress,* originally published in Great Britain, South African Niki Daly (1999), altered the representational style slightly toward a more exaggerated cartoon-style of facial features and other forms to complement his touchingly humorous story. Young Jamela, whose imaginative fascination with her mother's beautiful new dress material carries her away, prances down the street wrapped in yards of cloth, accompanied by children's chants of, "Kwela Jamela African Queen!" Of course, the results are disastrous, the material is ruined, her mother is terribly upset, and Jamela is contrite. However, a prize-winning photograph of Jamela saves the day and ensures a happy ending. Bright designs of local fabrics add cultural flavor throughout the story and on the front endpaper.

Impressionistic art, on the other hand, is much more evocative, portraying "the changing effect of light on surfaces at different times of day and under different atmospheric conditions" (Stewig, 1995, p. 193). Harvey Stevenson's lush acrylic paintings for *The Tangerine Tree* (1995) impressionistically convey this poignant story by Jamaican-born U.S. resident Regina Hanson. Ida and her family tearfully say goodbye to her father, who leaves them in Jamaica for work in the United States. Ida is sure her father will never return, but he reassures her that he will and that he will be thinking about them every day he is gone. Ida gives him a bottle filled with juice from the fruit of their tangerine tree to warm him in cold, snowy New York. Soft images in tropical colors accompany the author's use of dialect in this bittersweet narrative.

Expressionism "is intended to highlight the form of the reality, the essential or structural quality of the reality" (Cianciolo, 1997, p. 29). Linda Sapport's glowing pastel drawings for Lynn Joseph's (1998) *Jump Up Time: A Trinidad Carnival Story* are vivid and somewhat abstract with well-defined outlines of figures and objects. Young Lily is impatient with the preparations for her older sister Christine's costume for the Children's Carnival. Lily wants to "play mas" at the street festival herself, but she is too little to participate. However, when it is time for stage-frightened Christine to jump up for the dance, Lily gives her sister the courage to perform. The illustrations express well "the artist's subjective, emotional response" (Cianciolo, 1997, p. 29) to Lily's experience.

Cat and Mouse, by Polish-born Tomek Bogacki (1996), also exemplifies expressionism. His experience as a sculptor shows its influence in the rounded animal figures in muted cool tones. In this endearing story, a curious little mouse and equally inquisitive little cat, who don't know better, wander away from their mothers, discover each other, and innocently decide to play together. When they return home, their siblings wonder how each could befriend the other, usually a mortal enemy. In the end, they are curious enough, too, and all the kittens and mice play together the next day. Simplified shapes and spare backgrounds well suit this animal fable celebrating living in harmony with differences.

Niki Daly

South African author-illustrator Niki Daly is neither female nor black, although he is sometimes mistaken for both. The unusual spelling of his first name occurred after years of multiple spellings of his given name, Nikolaas (also, Nicolas and Nicholas). As an art student, Daly decided to end the confusion by using Niki as his first name, which created new ambiguities about his gender. Then, because he effectively portrays the black South African experience in some of his books, readers may assume that he is black, although his heritage actually is Irish, English, and Afrikaner (*Something about the Author Autobiography Series*, 1996).

Daly's route to children's book writing and illustrating was indirect, despite his evident talent as a child for drawing caricatures and his training at the Cape Technikon Art School in the 1960s. He began his artistic career with an advertising agency but became more interested in pursuing fame and fortune as a professional singer, which led him to England in 1971. That vocation did not succeed, but he did return to illustrating—both for an agency and as a freelancer. In London, he married Jude Daly (also from South Africa and a children's book illustrator—see Stewart's *Gift of the Sun: A Tale from South Africa* [1996] described in Chapter 5) and acquired his agent, Laura Cecil. Finally, in 1980, the Dalys felt compelled to return to South Africa at a time of political turmoil there as apartheid entered its final brutal years.

Daly credits Maurice Sendak, Harold Jones, and Edward Ardizzone with influencing his artistic style and characterizes himself as more of a drawer than a painter. As noted in the description of *Jamela's Dress*, his early interest in cartoon art also shows in the illustrations for this book. However, in other works, such as *Why the Sun and Moon Live in the Sky* (1995) and *Bravo, Zan Angelo! A Commedia Dell'Arte Tale* (1998), the influence of his trips to Italy, where he viewed Italian Renaissance art, appears.

Two noteworthy thematic strands stand out in Daly's work: ones that "evolve around young children . . . as they play around the home and on little excursions outside their home" (Telgen, 1994, p. 50) and ones that "honour children's rights . . . free of sexism and racism" (SAAAS, 1996, p. 92). One of his mostly widely known and successful titles, *Not So Fast, Songololo* (1986), about a young black boy's shopping trip with his grandmother (Goggo), exemplifies the unity of these two themes. It is also his most controversial work, particularly for the way he depicts Goggo in the illustrations. Some readers of all races see her size as offensive, while others (also of various ethnicities) view her as "a symbol of maternal love" (SAAAS, 1996, p. 90).

As well-known as Daly is for his own work, in South Africa he has been a major force behind indigenous children's book publishing. After the publication of *Songololo*, Daly convinced David Philip Publishers of South Africa to start a line of children's books, which Daly edited and named Songololo Books. In this capacity, and even later after a new editor succeeded him, Daly has developed, promoted, and advised many South African children's writers and illustrators regarding their careers, sometimes to the detriment of his own time for creative work. Thus, he has greatly influenced the world of children's literature not only through the books he authors and/or illustrates, but also through his support of the growing South African field of publishing.

Naive art is characterized by "simplification of what is seen and experienced, vitality and often awkward spontaneity, candidness and intensity" (Cianciolo, 1997, p. 32). Durga Bernhard's gouache paintings for Jane Kurtz's (1997) *Trouble* have naive qualities, especially the use of frontal and profile postures of the characters and flat, unshaded colors for skin and hair tones. This tale, one that the American author heard as a child in Ethiopia, is about the trouble that always finds Tekleh, a boy entrusted to watch his family's goats. One day when Tekleh sets off with the goats and a *gebeta* game to keep himself out of mischief, he meets a group of traders who ask for his wooden game board to make a fire. One thing leads to another with surprisingly happy results for a boy who always seems on the verge of disaster. Endpapers map the sequence of events in this playful, circular narrative.

Canadian resident Luis Garay (illustrator for Monica Hughes's [1993] *A Handful of Seeds* set in a Central American barrio) employs a modified naive style in *Pedrito's Day* (1997), set in his native Nicaragua. Simplified, static shapes and distinctly separated colors are shaded with cross-hatching in this story about Pedrito, a young boy who lives with his mother and grandmother and whose father has "gone North to work." Every day Pedrito shines shoes at the market where his mother sells tortillas and tamales to earn money for his family and to save for a new bicycle. One day when he runs an errand for Tía Paula, Pedrito loses her money, which he has to replace with his earnings. However, that same day, money arrives from his father—enough to pay the rent and put aside some for Pedrito's bicycle.

"In cartoon sketches the artist resorts to such techniques as slapstick, exaggerations, and absurdities depicting incongruities and incompatible characteristics or situations . . . " (Cianciolo, 1997, p. 36). British author-illustrator Lauren Child provides plenty of humor in her cartoon-like pictures for *I Want a Pet* (1999), originally published in Great Britain. In this story, a child begs for a pet, but every kind she suggests—a lion, sheep, wolf, octopus, boa constrictor, or bat—raises objections from her parents and grandparents. Finally, at the pet store, the girl finds the "perfect" solution—an egg that hasn't hatched yet. However, only when it does hatch will its species be revealed. Childlike black-line drawings with primary colors enhance the zaniness of this wishful romp.

Finally, Valeri Gorbachev, Ukrainian emigré to the United States, created cartoon-like illustrations for *Nicky and the Big, Bad Wolves* (1998). A young rabbit sleeping with four siblings yells for his mother when a nightmare about being chased by wolves wakens him. Nicky claims there were a hundred wolves, but instead of disputing whether the wolves were real, Nicky's mother merely questions the number of wolves until it is reduced to five. That still doesn't satisfy her terrified children, and ultimately, she chases them away by banging her broom on the trash bins and reassuringly snuggles between her young ones in bed. Wild eyes, exaggerated fangs, comical chase scenes, and printed sound effects all fit the "Road Runner" feel of the story.

Cultural Information

Picture book illustrations reveal cultural information in at least two ways: through the style of art used and through the content of the pictures. In the first case, many illustrators consciously incorporate artistic elements or styles that reflect the culture being depicted (Kiefer, 1995). Often these cultural borrowings are defined as folk art, which expresses "identifiable traditions, motifs, symbols, treatment of line, modeling, color, volume, and space" (Cianciolo, 1997, p. 33).

This type of art is common in illustrations for folktales but also is evident in many other picture books.

For example, in Tony Johnston's (1997) *Day of the Dead*, Jeanette Winter used Mexican folk art motifs to illustrate a family's preparations for *El día de los muertos*: making *empanadas, tamales,* and *mole,* picking fruit, grinding *chiles,* baking bread of the dead, cutting sugarcane, and creating marigold bouquets. On the festival night, they join their neighbors in a candlelight procession to the graveyard, where they place all the things they have made and joyously celebrate the lives of their dead loved ones. The pictures' border decorations and glowing acrylic colors all enhance the simple account of this Mexican tradition.

George Crespo's illustrations for Jonathan London's (1996) *The Village Basket Weaver* also consciously reflect the story's Belize setting. Young Tavio loves to watch his grandfather, Carpio, make baskets for the village and to listen to his stories about the old days. Tavio worries about how old Carpio is and whether he has the strength to continue his work, and Tavio begins to copy his grandfather's techniques. Finally, when Carpio is dying, he tells Tavio how to finish the cassava basket he is too weak to complete, and thus, the role of village basket weaver passes to Tavio. The artist explains how he researched the illustrations for this book by traveling to the Caribbean territory of the story, where he absorbed the culture and took classes on basket weaving under the master weaver. Not only do the illustrations reflect the village setting and inhabitants through color and detail, but each page of text or picture has a basket motif border.

As noted in previous book descriptions, pictorial content also can reveal substantial information about a culture. Some of this information requires readers and viewers to examine the illustrations closely to locate such clues. For example in British author Michael Rosen's (1999) *Rover* (first published by Bloomsbury in Great Britain), British illustrator Neal Layton incorporates several telling cultural details. This lighthearted romp uses role reversal to create humor. A dog is the narrator, who has a pet human named Rover and her parents, Rex and Cindy. The dog describes their daily activities and an outing to "an enormous sandpit" (the beach), where Rover wanders off by herself and the dog narrator helps the frantic humans find her. The illustrations are childlike pencil drawings and show the driver of the "family box" (car) on the right side (as done in the U.K.) and the television with an antenna not typical in the United States.

Likewise, Maja Dusíková, born in Czechoslovakia and a current resident of Italy, created a distinctly European setting for *Good-Bye, Vivi!,* by German author Antonie Schneider (1998) and first published by Nord-Süd Verlag AG in Switzerland. When Granny comes to live with Molly and Will, she brings along her cheerful canary, Vivi. The bird adds joy to all their lives with her singing, cheeping, and fluttering. However, both Granny and Vivi soon begin to show their old age—Granny by slowing down and staying indoors, Vivi by not eating and by sleeping more. When Vivi dies, they tenderly bury her in the garden, and later when Granny also dies, the whole family cries. Their sadness is eased with the discovery of a book Granny created filled with pictures and stories of her and Vivi's lives. Through the house windows, viewers can clearly see scenes of an old European town with closely clustered houses, steep roofs, and small-paned windows in the muted watercolor paintings.

Finally, American Ronald Himler captures the horror of war in his illustrations for *The Roses in My Carpets,* by Rukhsana Khan (1998), born in Pakistan and now living in Canada. In this sobering story, a refugee boy from Afghanistan relives in his dreams the terror of bombings that he, his mother, and sister escaped and that killed his farmer father. The narrator attends school and works as an apprentice carpet weaver. He tries to recapture some beauty by the colors he chooses and the roses he weaves into his carpet as a symbol of hope even after his sister is injured by a truck in the narrow streets. Himler's pictures depict the clothing; style of buildings; narrow streets filled with animals, people, and vehicles; meals eaten and lessons learned while squatting on the mud floor or on rough mats; the muezzin calling believers to prayer; and the interior of the clinic where the boy's sister is tended.

International Author-Illustrator Collaborations

Finally, picture book creation today increasingly involves authors and illustrators from different countries working together. Several titles reviewed previously already exemplify this trend, but additional examples further demonstrate it. One publisher, in particular—North-South Books, with its sister company, Nord-Süd Verlag—frequently brings together pairs of multinational authors and artists.

For example, Italian author Serena Romanelli and her Dutch husband, illustrator Hans de Beer, collaborate on the *Little Bobo* (1995) books. In *Little Bobo Saves the Day* (1997), the little orangutan likes to visit Uncle Darwin, whose cave is filled with fascinating objects from his travels around the world. Uncle Darwin always takes time to do and make things with Bobo, but he also warns Bobo to stay away from humans. However, when Uncle Darwin becomes ill, Bobo decides he must find some humans to get medicine. The first human Bobo encounters is young and just as nervous about orangutans as Bobo is about humans. They quickly realize they have nothing to fear from each other, and Pico takes Bobo to his home where there is medicine for Uncle Darwin. Before Bobo leaves, he and Pico exchange gifts of friendship. As in *Cat and Mouse,* this story carries a strong theme of not fearing differences.

Ragged Bear (1996) brings together author Brigitte Weninger from Austria and illustrator Alan Marks from England. This tender story is reminiscent of Don Freeman's (1968) *Corduroy* or Margery Williams's classic (1922) *The Velveteen Rabbit.* An old teddy bear usually sits forgotten in a corner, until he is brought to the park one day and left there when a rainstorm starts. Another child discovers him in a trash barrel and takes him home, where he is washed, dried, repaired, and loved. Charming watercolor illustrations perfectly complement the timeless narrative.

Look Out, Cinder! (1996) is a third North-South international collaboration. Author Dorothea Lachner from Austria and artist Eugen Sopko, born in the former Czechoslovakia and now living in Germany, combined efforts to create a story about a little black cat named Cinder, who lives alone in a big city. One night, fleeing from a huge red monster (a firetruck), Cinder hides in a delivery truck that takes her to an unfamiliar neighborhood. When Cinder starts to explore her new surroundings, she is harassed by three local cats, who all have staked out their territories. Still, Cinder follows the cats around and copies their actions, although they ignore her until one night when the red monster returns, sending Cinder fleeing in terror. As she is frantically about to leap from a wall into the yard below where there is a fierce dog, the other three cats yowl at her to stop. In spite of themselves, they have grown to care for the tiny cat. The scale of the full and double-spread illustrations emphasizes Cinder's small size and vulnerability. The pictures also contain cultural clues in the decidedly European streetscapes and building interiors.

Finally, Belgian author Cornette and French illustrator Rochette collaborated for *Purple Coyote* (1999), originally published by Pastel in France. This surrealistic fantasy portrays a boy named Jim who lives in a house "in the middle of a flat and arid desert." There he plays alone with a truck near a hill made of sand and rock until one day when a purple coyote appears on the hill. The coyote's unusual color, his dance, and his strange howl arouse Jim's curiosity. Before long, Jim asks the coyote about his color and is told that it is a secret. After several unsuccessful attempts to learn the secret, in frustration, Jim mimics the coyote's dance and howl. Immediately, Jim turns purple, the coyote's normal color is restored, and the grateful animal disappears. However, when Jim tries to pass off his secret curse to an approaching racoon, that creature refuses the bait. This cautionary story draws upon and updates the traditions of trickster tales from across many cultures.

This section demonstrates that the world of contemporary picture books offers opportunities to expand global horizons through their dual verbal and visual "languages." Young readers can glean many cultural insights from the content of both stories and pictures, illustration styles, and learning about the multinational authors and illustrators who create these books. Teachers can engage children in study of illustrators, artistic styles, the relationship of culture and artistic style, and comparisons of illustrations and styles within and between cultures. All of these facets increase children's artistic sophistication and their visual literacy, a topic we explore in greater depth in Chapter 5.

Fiction

Fiction for children encompasses fantasy (including science fiction) and realism (both contemporary and historical). These are works by known authors (as opposed to stories in the oral tradition), and little fiction was written specifically for children before the eighteenth century. In this section, after a brief historical and contemporary overview, we review selected recently published global fiction titles.

Many eighteenth- and nineteenth-century works of fiction for children read by American audiences were international. *Hans Brinker, or the Silver Skates* by American Mary Mapes Dodge (1865/1975) has a Dutch setting, while Johanna Spyri's beloved (1880) *Heidi* takes place in Switzerland, and *The Swiss Family Robinson* (1812/1949) is by Swiss author Johann David Wyss. British authors Robert Louis Stevenson and Lewis Carroll (Charles Dodgson) contributed *Treasure Island* (1883/1981) and *Alice's Adventures in Wonderland* (1865/1989), respectively, and from France came Jules Verne's *Twenty Thousand Leagues Under the Sea* (1869/1995). Early twentieth-century contributions included more works by British authors: Rudyard Kipling's (1902/1996) *Just So Stories*, Kenneth Grahame's (1908/1961) *The Wind in the Willows*, J. M. Barrie's (1906) *Peter Pan in Kensington Gardens*, and

A. A. Milne's (1926) *Winnie the Pooh*. Frances Hodgson Burnett's books, including the highly popular *The Secret Garden* (1911/1988), have English settings, while L. M. Montgomery's (1908/1983) *Anne of Green Gables* hails from Canada.

Several non-American Hans Christian Andersen Award winners are known relatively well to audiences in the United States. The Pippi Longstocking books by Astrid Lindgren from Sweden are widely read, and Tove Jansson from Finland is known to U.S. readers for the Moomintroll books. Swede Maria Gripe's Hugo and Josephine trilogy and Australian Patricia Wrightson's books have been published in the United States. Israeli author Uri Orlev has a strong American audience, as author also of three Mildred Batchelder Award winners. Additional familiar Batchelder

Uri Orlev

Israeli author Uri Orlev received the 1996 Hans Christian Andersen Award, and three of his books received the Mildred L. Batchelder Award: *The Island on Bird Street* (1984), *The Man from the Other Side* (1991), and *The Lady with the Hat* (1995). In September, 1998, a movie based on *The Island on Bird Street* previewed on Showtime. Orlev writes in Hebrew, although this is not his native language.

He was born in Warsaw, Poland, in 1931 and was a child during the Nazi occupation of Poland and persecution of the Jews. During the war, Orlev lived in the Warsaw ghetto and was then sent to the Bergen-Belsen concentration camp. His mother was killed by the Germans during the war and his father was a Russian prisoner. After his mother's death in 1943, his Aunt Stefa cared for him and his younger brother and the three of them survived the war, as did his father. In 1945, Orlev and his brother emigrated to Palestine (i.e., Israel) where he finished school and served in the army. Although he spent many years on a kibbutz, he has lived in the Yemin Moshe neighborhood of Jerusalem since 1968. Orlev is married and has four children and two grandchildren.

Orlev's books that have been translated into English by his friend, Hillel Halkin, are novels about the Holocaust and its aftermath. In reflecting on this time in his life, Orlev has written: " I don't know if writing about the past helps me to get over it. What I do know is that

there is no grown-up way to talk, tell, or think about the things that happened to me. I have to remember them as if I were still a boy . . . As a grown-up, I can't imagine my own children living through what I did" (1998, p. 56).

Orlev began writing poetry as a boy hiding in the Warsaw ghetto and continued writing in Bergen-Belsen, where he decided to become a writer. His first book was for adults, the autobiographical novel *The Lead Soldiers* (1956 in Israel; 1979 in the United States). He has written over 25 books for children, although only four have been translated into English. Orlev also writes scripts for radio, television, and movies and translates Polish books into Hebrew.

Orlev's work is critically acclaimed, and his books have been translated into 15 languages. In a 1997 interview, Orlev discussed his books' universal appeal to children: "I think it is a good story. We are writing all the time about the same thing, love, war, jealousy. If the story is good, children will want to read it" (Freeman, 1999, p. 45). His stories affirm the value of children's imagination and their ability to survive the most difficult circumstances. The Andersen Award jury expressed: "His stories have integrity and humour, while his characters learn a loving, accepting attitude towards others—the lesson of how to accept being different in an alien world" (as cited in Khorana, 1996, p. 8).

winners include *Friedrich* (1970/1987) by Hans Peter Richter of Germany, *The Boys from St. Petri* (1994) by Danish author Bjarne Reuter, *The Friends* (1996) by Kazumi Yumoto of Japan, and German Josef Holub's (1997) *The Robber and Me*.

American children also know the work of other contemporary international authors: masterpieces of suspense by Margaret Mahy from New Zealand (twice winner of Britain's prestigious Carnegie Medal); British authors Roald Dahl's zany fantasies, Brian Jacques's animal fantasies, and Alan Garner's high fantasies; Sheila Gordon's realistic South African novels; Japanese-born Kyoto Mori's poignant *Shizuko's Daughter* (1993); and Jean Little's numerous stories from Canada.

Most of the recently published fictional titles that we include here are serious in tone, and many are young-adult books. They are clustered into the following themes: facing and conquering personal struggles; children coping with survival on their own; the impact of war, violence, and racial prejudice on children's and their families' lives; coming to terms with death of a loved one; and learning to understand persons from other cultures. We believe that through discussions of themes such as these and others, teachers can facilitate children's literary development, a topic we explore more specifically through genre study in Chapter 5. Finally, we briefly explore the issue of cultural taboos, since some fiction especially presents controversial elements for readers.

Personal Struggles

Personal struggles for young people can be wide-ranging: many involve coping with family problems, making choices for oneself, or finding one's identity. In some cultures, for example, the range of choices that girls or women have about whom to marry and the direction of their lives after marriage is restricted, as demonstrated in the following two books. Nancy Farmer's IBBY honor novel, *A Girl Named Disaster* (1996), is set in Mozambique in the early 1980s. Eleven-year-old Nhamo, whose mother was killed by a leopard and whose father has returned to his native Zimbabwe, is betrothed to a much older man with three wives. Feeling desperately unloved and unaccepted in her own village, Nhamo decides to flee and try to find her way to her father. She sets out alone on the Musengezi River, but her canoe is swept into the terrifying Lake Cabora Bassa. To survive, she joins a baboon troop on an island, eventually escapes, and continues her perilous journey to her father's family home in Zimbabwe. Along the way, she communicates with her dead mother and ancestors, meets people who both befriend and threaten her, and conquers her fears in this gripping survival saga. Readers gain valuable insights into Shona cultural customs, the beliefs of the African spirit religion, and even the political history of southeastern Africa. A "cast of characters," maps, a glossary, information about the historical background of the region and belief system of the Shona, and a bibliography help readers follow this complex story.

Korean-born Helen Kim also uses the voice of an 11-year-old protagonist, Junehee Lee, in her National Book Award finalist *The Long Season of Rain* (1996) to offer a child's perspective on her mother's unhappy married life. Gradually, Junehee comes to understand the severe constraints imposed upon her mother, whose entire life is dictated by her husband and his mother. When Junehee's mother decides to keep an orphaned boy against her husband's wishes, the entire household enters a crisis that is resolved only when Junehee's mother takes a bold step of leaving the family for a period of time. Set in Korea in the 1960s, this novel offers insights into a time and culture that further stimulate thoughts about asserting oneself and accepting reality. The book's focus on the mother's marriage and personal struggles make this a more mature read than the narrator's age would otherwise suggest. The symbol of *changma*, the long rainy season, provides an underlying thread of the multiple changes that occur in an eventful year.

An unnamed teenage girl is the first-person narrator of *Checkers* (1998) by one of Australia's most acclaimed authors, John Marsden. In this gripping contemporary novel, the girl recounts, from her mental hospital setting, the breaking scandal of her powerful father's shady business practices. His dealings, which appear to have been going on for years, have made their upscale lifestyle possible and involve collusion with the government. Finally, when he acquires a government-awarded casino contract, the opposition party and media begin to investigate the whole unethical operation. Ironically, a dog that the girl's father gives her and she names Checkers (unaware of the historical significance of Richard Nixon's namesake pet) plays a part in the final piece of evidence that leads to the scheme's exposure. The narrative is told in a series of flashbacks, interspersed with the girl's current experiences in the hospital, where she is sent after a nervous breakdown from her undeserved guilt over her father's demise and the fate of her dog.

Award-winning Canadian author, Tim Wynne-Jones, explores the dark side of family secrets in *Stephen Fair* (1998). The 15-year-old protagonist, for whom the book is titled, is beginning to have the same nightmare that drove his older brother from home four years before: a village of treehouses, a terrible fire threatening the village, a baby crying, and himself trying to rescue the baby. His mother, fearing the same loss of her younger son, tries to convince Stephen to accept alternative treatment from a practitioner of "applied kinesiology." Stephen resists, however, convinced that each nightmare is gradually bringing him closer to unlocking the mystery of his family's unusual past and his own childhood. Meanwhile, Stephen makes friends with a classmate and neighbor, Virginia, who has her own family problems to solve. Their friendship provides both humor and poignancy as the plot progresses. Powerful images of fire and water and the metaphor of life as a movie recur throughout the narrative, providing strong reinforcement for important themes of destruction, rebirth, and facing and living reality. The unique symbol of a "trick cyclist" (a wordplay on "psychiatrist") suggests the importance of resolving one's own issues, which Stephen does with considerable enterprise to create a satisfying conclusion.

Flour Babies (1994) by British author Anne Fine portrays the metaphorical "rebirth" of an unforgettable character, Simon Martin, the biggest and most feared of the academic and social misfits who comprise Mr. Cassidy's special class for underachievers and troublemakers at St. Boniface School. This group is assigned an experiment for the school science fair: to care for 6-pound sacks of flour as if they were real babies for 3 weeks. Simon unexpectedly becomes attached to his flour baby and undergoes a transformation as he learns the responsibilities of parenthood, an understanding that provides him with insight about his own father's desertion when Simon was 6 weeks old. Although in the end Simon remains essentially himself, this humorous contemporary novel, winner of England's prestigious Carnegie Medal, presents a noteworthy example of character development. The book's worthwhile themes are presented with a light touch, much hilarity, a fast pace, and thoroughly British tone.

Similarly, Scottish author J. K. Rowling has created the unforgettable character of Harry Potter, whose personal struggles are featured in her fantasy novels about him. When readers first meet Harry in *Harry Potter and the Sorcerer's Stone* (1998; originally published by Bloomsbury Publishing of London in 1997 under the title *Harry Potter and the Philosopher's Stone*), he is an orphan living with his mean aunt and uncle and his most unpleasant cousin, characters reminiscent of Roald

Dahl's. When Harry is 11 years old, he learns that he is a wizard and by a series of magical events is transported to Hogwarts School of Witchcraft and Wizardry. Here, Harry forms wonderful friendships and experiences exciting adventures. In the fine tradition of British fantasy, Rowling has created a highly imaginative novel and makes it easy for readers to "believe the unbelievable" and "great, good fun for them to do so" (Gray, 1999, p. 69).

Finally, in well-known Canadian Jean Little's historical fiction, *The Belonging Place* (1997), young Elspet Mary loses her mother in an accident on the streets of Aberdeen, Scotland, one day in 1835. Downstairs neighbors keep her until her sailor father returns and takes Elspet Mary to live with her aunt and uncle's family in the small village of Glen Buchan. They accept her as one of their own children, and later she legally becomes their daughter when her father's ship is wrecked at sea. However, just when Elspet Mary feels as though she belongs, her family begins to discuss moving to Canada, where more land is available. Eventually, they do that and soon find new neighbors who have reluctantly taken in a baby boy whose parents died from cholera. When Elspet Mary witnesses how the neighbor, Mrs. Mackay, resents the child (since her own son died from the same disease), she loses her sense of security with her adoptive family, until her mother lovingly reassures Elspet Mary how much she is wanted. The parallel motifs of belonging in an adopted family and an adopted country highlight the need for home and love that children everywhere feel and illuminate the universal immigrant experience.

Struggle to Survive

Survival stories are a universal literary motif, and ones about children struggling to survive without adult assistance can range from the romantic to the grimly realistic. Toward the romantic side lies Stephen Menick's folktale-like *The Muffin Child* (1998), set in 1913 in "an old country in the Balkans" (p. 3). This haunting story features 11-year-old Tanya, whose parents are swept away by a flooded river while she alone was spared. Believing that they remain alive somehow, she refuses to leave her family's farm to live with people in the village. She is determined to survive on her own and take care of the farm and the cow, Milenka, for her parents' eventual return. To support herself, she discovers that she can make and sell muffins to the villagers and passing travelers. Gradually, she faces her own guilt and anger for her parents' disappearance and gains a new perspective on their final actions. Tanya also learns that she cannot trust the villagers, who want to take the farm away from her for their own gain, or Anton the Sharpener, who seems to befriend her but turns out to be sinister. Only the gypsies, who camp on her land and whom the villagers despise and tell her to fear, turn out to be her true saviors. The primary narrative is presented as a story told by a mother to her daughter about her great-grandmother, who emigrated with the gypsies to the United States.

Asphalt Angels by Ineke Holtwijk (1999) starkly portrays the life of Alex, a homeless boy in Rio de Janeiro. When his foster mother dies, her husband throws Alex out of the house. For awhile he lives in a park along the beach, and, feeling all alone even among other homeless persons, he calls himself Crusoe after Robinson

Crusoe. The street's dangers are myriad, from simple hunger and the threat of starvation to sexual predators and street gangs. Eventually, Alex joins a gang, the Asphalt Angels, for the relative security of group protection. Most of their lives are occupied with the need to subsist and the despair of ever realizing a brighter future, but in the midst of such circumstances the beauty of positive human relationships still shines. Although Alex refuses to take drugs as the others do to escape their existence, he can't avoid becoming involved in other crimes such as stealing in order to survive, for which one scheme turns tragic. This book contains graphic images of violence, drug use, and sexuality, which may pose issues for American audiences. The author, a correspondent in Latin America for Dutch newspapers and television, based this story on her experiences in Brazil and provides additional information in an afterword about the lives of the street children she learned to know. In an ironic sidelight, the media plays an important and mostly negative role in Alex's story. A glossary explains unfamiliar terms and names.

War, Violence, and Prejudice

Many children from around the world feel the impact of war, violence, and racial, ethnic, or religious prejudice on their lives and the lives of their families and friends. Kathy, a young South African girl in Dianne Case's *92 Queens Road* (1995), begins to develop an awareness of racial discrimination and what it means to grow up "Coloured" there in the 1960s. She lives with an extended family that includes her grandmother (Ma), her mother who works long hours in a clothing factory, and Uncle Reggie, when he is on shore leave as a sailor. Their neighborhood includes a vibrant mixture of cultures, religions, and customs. Other uncles, aunts, and cousins visit frequently, including one uncle whose family passes for white and lives in a much finer neighborhood. Kathy and her family watch the painful displacement of a nearby neighborhood under the government's policy of "forced removals" and face daily acts of discrimination, both large and small. This insider's story, based upon the author's own experiences of growing up in Cape Town, helps to put into perspective the momentous events of recent years with the collapse of apartheid. Meanwhile, readers glimpse everyday events in lives of another time and culture, thereby perhaps gaining a sense of human universality as well as uniqueness. This novel received South Africa's Sir Percy Fitzpatrick Prize for Literature.

On another continent, 17-year-old Juan lives in poverty with his family in Bogotá, Colombia, in Lyll Becerra de Jenkins's contemporary novel, *So Loud a Silence* (1996). With a typically rebellious teenage attitude, Juan disdains his father and feels out of place in his family, so he is sent to visit his grandmother, a landowner in the countryside. For decades, an ongoing war between the army and guerrillas has been waging, and in some areas the *campesinos* (farmers) have been victimized in the middle. However, Juan's grandmother and the other landowners in her region have managed so far to avoid the conflict by remaining nonpolitical. While staying with her, Juan decides to assert himself by becoming involved with a group of young people, led by an outside agitator, who are determined to form their own guerrilla force. The results of his actions pose grave risks to Juan and his grandmother, and Juan gains painful understanding about the importance of family ties and about his own identity. This provocative novel offers a chance for readers to learn more about Colombia's political history and to consider the conflicts that sometimes ensue between the idealism of youth and other worthwhile values. The author, a native of Colombia, now lives in the United States.

The horrors of World War II have prompted many books for young people in the years since its conclusion. Donna Jo Napoli's *Stones in Water* (1997) was inspired by a friend's wartime experiences as a boy in Venice, Italy. One day at a movie theater, German soldiers round up Roberto, his friend, Samuele, and other boys (who are still in middle school) and transport them by train to become forced laborers at Nazi work camps. Their treatment is inhumane and the working conditions brutal, but their circumstances could be even worse if the Nazis discover that Samuele is Jewish. At the work camp in Germany, they find other prisoners in a separate area who are Jewish and who are near starvation. Roberto begins to befriend a Jewish girl by sneaking food to her through the fence, and she gives him a special stone in return before the boys are shipped to another work camp in Ukraine. Samuele (called Enzo to protect his identity) sustains their spirits with the stories he tells. However, after Enzo dies from a beating by other inmates, Roberto decides to escape and eventually links up with an Italian soldier deserter. They make their way to safety and both join the *partigiana*, resisters against the war. In the end, Roberto shares the girl's gift stone and Enzo's stories with his new companion as a way of passing on their legacy. This novel offers yet another glimpse of how the lives of many different kinds of people were affected by a terrible war.

In German author Gudrun Pausewang's grim account, *The Final Journey* (1996) originally published in Germany, Anna, an 11-year-old Jewish girl, embarks on a forced journey with her grandfather from Nazi Germany to an unknown destination. The pair loses Grandmother on their way to the train station and finds themselves jammed into a railway cattle truck with dozens of other people. In the train, lacking amenities, initially awful conditions deteriorate rapidly, and layer by layer, Anna's innocence is stripped away as she gradually realizes the truth that her parents (who had disappeared earlier) and grandparents had managed to shield from her during years of hiding. The entire story takes place on the train to Auschwitz, interspersed with her memories of a happily normal life before this terrible tragedy, and ends with Anna preparing for the new arrivals' "shower." Graphic narrative and horrifying events make this historical novel an unforgettable, if wrenching, experience suitable only for very mature readers. However, it offers a most compelling view of the Holocaust and gives readers a disturbing immediacy through Anna's perspective.

Death

Unfortunately, coming to terms with the death of a loved one is an issue that many young people around the world have had to face. Swedish authors Peter Pohl and Kinna Gieth explore this theme in *I Miss You, I Miss You* (1999), winner of the

I Miss You, I Miss You! © 1992 by Peter Pohl & Katarina Gieth. Used with permission of the publisher, R & S Books.

Swedish August Prize and the German Children's Literature Prize. Based upon Gieth's own experience, this novel portrays 13-year-old identical twin girls, Tina and Cilla, with their typical (and contrasting) interests and conflicts with parents until one day when Cilla is killed by a car as she is running to catch the school bus. Tina is devastated not only by the loss of her soulmate, but also by the unnerving reactions of others around her who see Cilla's reflection in her. Tina struggles with an identity crisis, compounded by the guilt (for safely crossing the road ahead of Cilla) and fear she feels about Cilla's death. She also falls in love with a boy at the drama camp both she and Cilla had planned to attend together. In the end, Tina gains a new sense of herself and a more mature perspective on life. The narrative realistically conveys the stages of grief and coping with life after death; it also includes adolescent language and sexuality that may be outside the comfort level of some American readers. However, it is a moving portrayal of one girl's year of recovery from loss and discovery of who she truly is. Its themes are relevant to teenagers everywhere, even if their individual experiences differ.

Something Very Sorry (1996) is based upon the actual experience of 9-year-old Rosemyn, as written by her father, Arno Bohlmeijer from the Netherlands. Shortly before Christmas, Rosemyn and her family are in a car accident that results in her mother's death and her father's and younger sister's serious injuries. Her own emotional injuries are more serious than her physical ones: Rosemyn blames her father for not watching the road carefully when he was driving, thus killing her mother, and she fears for the recovery of her father and sister. The narrative begins with the accident on December 13 and ends January 7 when the three surviving family members go home. It is told in first-person voice through dated entries, like a diary, in the appropriately simple language of a young child, whose heartbreak and bewilderment over what has happened are universal childhood emotions. The story is all the more poignant because it is true.

Intercultural Understanding

Contact with persons from other cultures is unavoidable in today's shrinking globe, and in many regions it is a facet of everyday life. Such contact should be enriching, but books also explore the frictions that can arise along the way to understanding and acceptance. In *The Storyteller's Beads* (1998), Jane Kurtz, who grew up in Ethiopia and now lives in the United States, portrays the misunderstanding between two minority religious groups in Ethiopia—the Beta-Israel, as Ethiopian Jews call themselves, or Falasha (meaning Stranger), as others call them, and the Kemant, a sect that blends Christianity, Judaism, and spirit worship. Both groups are oppressed by the dominant Amhara, but the Beta-Israel are considered beneath everyone. The story is set in the 1980s, when war with Eritrea and famine caused persecuted ethnic groups such as the Kemant and Beta-Israel to flee to refugee camps in neighboring Sudan. Two girls, Sahay (Kemant) and Rahel (Jewish), find themselves in the same group escaping to the Sudan and having to depend on each other when both girls lose all family members. At first, Sahay despises Rahel, who is blind, but Rahel has to depend on Sahay to be her guide. Rahel tells Sahay the ancient stories of the Jewish people, using the amber beads her grandmother gave her in order to remember them. Gradually, both girls overcome their prejudices and fears to become such close companions that after they reach the refugee camp, Rahel determines to take Sahay with her to Israel on one of the rescue flights sent by the Israeli government. Thus, no longer strangers to each other, the story of Nahomey (Naomi) and Hirute (Ruth) becomes their own story. Background historical information and a glossary enhance readers' background knowledge.

Habibi, by Naomi Shihab Nye (1997), is a contemporary novel about a bicultural Palestinian American family who decides to move from St. Louis, Missouri, to an apartment outside Jerusalem, near the father's home village. Liyana, age 14, is unhappy with the change, which means leaving behind the culture and friends she has known all her life. Everything is new and strange to Liyana in Israel, and the mixture of cultures is bewildering: Although Liyana feels American, she attends an Armenian girls' school and meets her Palestinian relatives, including her grandmother (Sitti) for the first time. She also meets a new friend, Omer, and only later realizes that he is Jewish. An altercation in a nearby Palestinian refugee camp brings the Palestinian-Israeli conflict into the life of Liyana's family and complicates Liyana's relationship with Omer. Eventually, however, she takes Omer to meet her Sitti, and Sitti's acceptance of Omer brings the blend of cultures into a healthy balance for Liyana. *Habibi*, which means "darling," comes to symbolize the love that Liyana feels in her new home. Each chapter begins with a title and a thought, such as Liyana would have written in her notebook and that foreshadow the chapter's contents.

Issues Related to Cultural Taboos

One thing that many American readers may notice particularly in books published abroad and imported to the United States is the different standards that authors from other countries may hold regarding such issues as strong language, sexuality, and bodily functions. As noted in several of the previous reviews, some international books contain language and explicit references to sexuality or bodily functions that some American audiences may find uncomfortable or even objectionable in books for young people. Likewise, there is material in books that we take for granted in this country but which would be problematic or unsuitable in other places (i.e., Moslem countries or communist China). These are issues related to cultural, religious, and even political taboos; what is acceptable or normal in one place may be shocking in another. However, if readers can be open-minded and remember the context of the literary work, such issues can be a means for learning about other ways of looking at life and an opportunity for intercultural understanding, which, after all, is the role that global literature should serve.

The titles described in this section sample global fiction available for young people in the United States. Some portray universal tasks of growing up, such as becoming independent, the search for one's identity, facing and accepting reality, being accepted for oneself, forming relationships, or the loss of innocence. These themes illuminate the common bonds of humanity and provide identification with other children and young adults around the world. Other books highlight unique experiences for particular readers or groups of people, sometimes due to cultural factors, sometimes due to circumstances that just happen, such as war, death, or homelessness. These novels broaden readers' horizons by exposure to different religions, political and cultural realities, or experiences and create empathy for others whose lives may differ markedly from their own. Both kinds of reading are important for literary and personal development.

Informational Books

The first informational book written especially for children dates back to 1657, when Moravian bishop John Amos Comenius wrote *Orbis Sensualium Pictus* ("The Visible World in Pictures"). Written in Latin and illustrated with woodcuts, this informational picture book presented natural history in a picture dictionary format. If we fast-forward to the United States, in 1919 Macmillan Company was the first publisher to begin a department that focused exclusively on children's books. Under the direction of Louise Seaman, Macmillan's Children's Books published some titles with global content. The first Newbery Medal was given to an informational book that also provided a global perspective, van Loon's *The Story of Mankind* (1921). Yet even with such a prominent history, informational books, as a genre, have not received the kind of attention and visibility afforded picture books and fiction in international children's literature. A landmark book appeared in 1980 with the publication of *People* by Peter Spier. This oversized informational picture book conveyed the strong message that people around the world share similarities, yet their differences should be praised and affirmed. Through text and detailed, colorful illustrations, Spier depicts the universals of culture as well as the distinctive aspects that make each culture unique. Since then, informational books imported from other countries and published within the United States that focus on global content have proliferated. In recent years, several trends have emerged in informational books within international children's literature. We discuss four of these trends in this section: series books, photo-essays, design and graphics, and the range of topics.

Series Books

Series books, in contrast to single-author titles, are initiated by a publishing company to provide a group of books linked by a common theme or subject. These books follow a specified format and are usually written by an author selected by the publisher.

Clearly, the leading publisher of informational children's books worldwide is the British publisher DK (Dorling Kindersley). This company was started in 1974 by Peter Kindersley and Christopher Dorling as publishers of informational books for adults. In 1987, it initiated its children's series and published *The Way Things Work* (1988) by David Macaulay. This best-selling work has sold over 2.4 million copies and has been translated into 19 languages. DK has its own bookstore in London that sells both adult and children's titles. In 1991 the company established DK Inc. to publish books in the United States. DK titles are popular in the United States and include such series as "Eyewitness Readers," "Stephen Biesty Incredible Books," "Look Inside Cross-Sections," "Young Enthusiast," and "Eyewitness Science." These books are characterized by their visually appealing presentation, which combines information with photographs and other graphics to help convey material, often in oversize format. In *Children Just Like Me* (1995), published in collaboration with UNICEF and written by Barnabas and Anabel Kindersley, readers meet children like themselves around the world. For example, a two-page spread features 10-year-old Bogna from Poland. A full-length color photograph of Bogna and her family are the center of the spread, surrounded by information about her family's farm, her school, and food she likes. Illustrations include smaller photographs as well as a page from a school notebook. Font size varies, and the text, not placed in a linear fashion, is interspersed across the pages with the illustrations.

Another popular British publisher of informational series books is Usborne Books distributed in the United States by Educational Development Corporation. Peter Usborne started this company in 1973, and now Usborne has over 800 titles in print. Similar to DK books, Usborne books are known for their appealing format. As its home page describes, "Usborne books use many ways to encourage children to study the illustrations and text rather than simply looking, such as strip cartoons, speech bubbles, hand lettering, cutaways, and diagrams." Usborne's many series include "Understanding Science," "Understanding Geography," "Famous Lives," and "Soccer School." In the "Soccer School" series, each title focuses on an aspect of soccer such as "Training and Fitness" and "Goalkeeping."

Another international publisher of nonfiction series books that has found popularity in the United States is the French publisher Editions Gallimard, whose books have been translated into English and distributed in the United States by Scholastic. The "First Discovery Books" are a small size—6¼ inches × 7⅛ inches—and geared for young children ages 3 to 7. They cover a range of topics from *Sports* by Valat (1998) to *Endangered Animals* by Perols (1997). The format of this series is interactive, featuring colorful illustrations and transparent overlays. For example, Jeuness and de Bourgoing's *The Egg* (1992), one of the first titles to appear in the United States, opens to a large brown egg on acetate paper with the words, "Here is an egg. Let's look inside!" In turning the acetate, the child is greeted on the next page by a colorful, realistic painting of the cross section of the egg. The book continues to inform young readers about where eggs come from, how the egg grows, and the different kinds of eggs.

Several U.S. publishers specialize in informational titles, and the number of series books has grown in recent years. While these books provide strong links to the curriculum and cover a wide range of topics, they usually follow a specific formula and format and therefore are not always of the same literary quality as single-subject titles. The Lerner Publishing Group, which includes Carolrhoda Books, produces many informational series with a focus on global issues. For example, the "Count Your Way" series by Jim Haskins uses a counting format to present information about various countries such as Brazil, the Arab World, Italy, and Israel. Several books in the series "Journey between Two Worlds" have been named a National Council for the Social Studies (NCSS) Notable Children's Trade Book: *A Russian Jewish Family* by Leder (1996); *A Bosnian Family* by Silverman (1997); and *A Guatemalan Family* by Malone (1996). In this series, a refugee family's life in their native country and their journey to the United States are told through color photographs as well as black and white historical photos. Similarly, "The World's Children" series provides photo-essays on the lives of children around the globe. Many of these titles have also been named to the NCSS notables list such as Goldsmith's *The Children of Mauritania* (1993) and Pitkänen's *The Grandchildren of the Vikings* (1996).

Photo-Essays

A second trend in international informational books is the photo-essay. Photographers from the United States and many nations of the world are sharing their craft through informative photo-essays for children. For example, award-winning Japanese photographer, Michio Hoshino, escorts children to the Alaskan wilderness in *The Grizzly Bear Family Book* (1994). Translated by Karen Calligan-Taylor and originally published in 1992 in Switzerland, this book recounts the author's own backpacking experience in Alaska through text and color photographs. The endpapers of the book feature a panoramic view of the snow-covered Alaskan wilderness with a lone bear in the foreground. Photographs and text work together as they would in a picture book, creating a unified whole. The first-person text gives readers a sense of a personalized view of the daily life of the grizzly bear and the environment in which she lives. The author's strong respect for his topic is evident as he writes, "No matter how many books you read, no matter how much television you watch, there is no substitute for experiencing nature firsthand. If you cannot meet a bear in the wild, then you must try to imagine it . . . "

This desire of photographers to experience firsthand and share their experience with children is evident throughout contemporary photo-essays written for children. American photographer and popular children's author of informational books George Ancona traveled with his family to Olinda, Brazil, to document *Carnaval* (1999), the five-day festival that precedes Lent. Ancona's photographs have illustrated more than 70 children's books and often focus on multicultural and global themes. In *Carnaval*, vibrant color photographs fill each page and parallel the text, which follows the preparations and celebration of the yearly carnaval in this small Brazilian city. Readers will be enthralled by photographs of the *benecos gigantes*, the giant puppets distinctive to this city. A "Note from the Author" provides further description of Olinda and the carnaval tradition.

Belgian photographer Victor Englebert collaborated with American author David M. Schwartz in *Yanomami: People of the Amazon* (1995). This sensitive photo-essay transports children to an endangered culture deep within the Amazon rain forest. Through full-page color photographs and text, daily life in a Yanomami village is revealed. A map of the "Lands of the Yanomami" shows their location between Venezuela and Brazil. An author's note provides further information about the Yanomami as an endangered culture. Finally, a section on "What You Can Do" indicates specific ideas for children who want to take action to save the Amazon rain forest and the Yanomami.

Design and Graphics (Format)

Informational books no longer resemble encyclopedias in format, with dense text and small illustrations. Today's informational books host a variety of formats, striking designs, and innovative use of graphics. *Tibet through the Red Box* (1998) by Czech-born author and artist Peter Sís exemplifies this trend. This oversized volume is 11 inches × 11 inches square and the intriguing, unusual cover itself signals a unique design. In the center of the cover is a square painting of a maze with a Tibetan mountain village in the middle. The translucent book jacket allows readers to see this maze through an overlay of brown line drawings of map symbols

Carñaval

GEORGE ANCONA

Reprinted with permission of Harcourt, Inc. © 1999.

and other objects conveying a journal and travel. The title and author's name are printed in large letters in red ink. The book begins as the author finds his father's locked red box that contains a diary of his father's filmmaking trip to Tibet during the 1950s to document the construction of a Himalayan highway. When the side of the mountain collapses, Sís's father is separated from the construction crew and chronicles the mysterious adventure he experiences, lost in Tibet for several months. Each page of this remarkable book is a visual feast with surprising elements. The diary's text is printed in black ink in a font that resembles a person's handwriting and contrasts the explanatory text by Sís printed in regular font. Color paintings completely fill several double-page spreads; diary pages are printed on parchment-like paper in contrast to the white pages of the text; and smaller drawings fill various nooks and crevices of pages. The design contributes to the book's mystical, ethereal quality.

Belgian film producer Litsa Boudalika facilitated the correspondence between two 12-year-old girls, Mervet, a Palestinian who lives in the Dheisheh refugee camp near Jerusalem, and Galit, an Israeli who lives in Jerusalem. The book, *If You Could Be My Friend* (1998; originally published by Gallimard Publications in 1992 as *Si Tu Veux Être Mon Amie*), is organized around the series of letters written by the girls from 1988 to 1991. The author has written a prelude to each letter, printed in italics, which explains a corresponding event in the Arab-Israeli conflict. The girls' meeting in Jerusalem on April 6, 1991, is described by the author. The last portion of the book, "Two Peoples and One Land: A Historical Overview" and a glossary of terms was written by Ariel Cohen. The book also includes a list of suggested readings and an index.

Another unique book format, *Learning to Swim in Swaziland: A Child's-Eye View of a Southern African Country* (1993), was written by Nina Leigh when she was 8 years old about the year her family spent in Swaziland. The book's design features many kinds of graphics. The text is printed in Nina's own handwriting, and illustrations include drawings that Nina created and color photographs. For example, on one page, Nina draws a map of a "homestead" and labels each item such as "husband's hut," "kitchen hut," and "fire." Each page offers a distinct design in terms of placement of text and illustrations as readers share Nina's experience. On the book's last page, Nina writes, "You should not be afraid of what you have never done. You can do all kinds of things you never dreamed you could do. Just like swimming. Just like writing a book. Just like living in Africa."

Since the publication of the Caldecott award–winning *Ashanti to Zulu: African Traditions* by Musgrove (1976), the ABC format has become popular in conveying information. With vivid paintings by Leo and Diane Dillon, this book described 26 different African tribes. More recently the British book, Onyefulu's *A Is for Africa* (1993), follows the alphabet format to present facts about the African continent. The author, born in Nigeria and currently living in England, explains in her author's note that "this alphabet is based on my own favorite images of the Africa I know." Each page highlights one letter of the alphabet, a short paragraph about the word, and a color photograph to illustrate the word. For instance, the book informs readers that C is for a Canoe, K is for Kola nuts, and T is for Turban.

Range of Topics

Informational books span a range of topics that focus on plant and animal life, contemporary cultures, the arts, and historical events. Frequently a book will explore a specific topic in depth rather than present a general survey. The survey approach is more frequently found in the series books. Individual authors often write books on topics that have personal meaning or importance to them.

The history of music is presented in the humorous book, *Long Live Music!* written and illustrated by Les Chat Pelés, three French artists (1996; originally published by Editions du Seuil in 1995 as *Vive la musique!*). In this oversized book, readers learn that "the oldest instruments ever found were Neolithic bone flutes" and that "traveling musicians brought music to the people" during the Middle Ages. Colorful, cartoon-like illustrations include labeled pictures of unusual instruments such as Peruvian panpipes and Iranian dulcimer and comic renditions to support the historical discussion.

Dolphin's *Neve Shalom/Wahat al-Salam: Oasis of Peace* (1993) presents an in-depth look at the special Arab-Jewish community in Israel where "Arabs and Jews of Israeli citizenship choose to live and work together equally and in peace" (p. 28). Nominated four times for the Nobel Peace Prize, this unique community opened enrollment in its school to children from outside the village. Color photographs by Ben Dolphin follow the lives of two 10-year-old boys, one Jewish and one Arab Moslem, whose parents do not live in the village but decide to send them to the school. The book also includes more information about Neve Shalom/Wahat al-Salam, a brief history of Israel, a glossary, and a page of Hebrew/Arabic Language Comparison.

Former zoo keeper Roland Smith and zoo veterinarian Michael J. Schmidt traveled to Myanmar (formerly Burma) to document *In the Forest with the Elephants* (1998), an informational book about the elephants who work to support the teak industry. Color captioned photographs taken by the authors support the text, which details the role of timber elephants and the men who ride them, called *oozies*. This fascinating account provides insight into a topic few American children would normally encounter in the traditional school curriculum, and as the book jacket notes, the story reveals "this working partnership between elephants and humans may be the key to preserving the elephants themselves as well as their forest home."

Award-winning American authors Patricia and Fredrick McKissack transport readers back to the Middle Ages in *The Royal Kingdoms of Ghana, Mali, and Songhay: Life in Medieval Africa* (1994). This carefully researched book focuses on Western African kingdoms of Mande-speaking groups. "They are a proud people, who know of a time when the great trading empires of Ghana, Mali, and Songhay flourished in their homeland" (p. xviii). Illustrated with maps, photographs, and reproductions of art, the book includes a time line, extensive notes, a bibliography, and index. The authors acknowledge the assistance of several scholars who specialize in archeology and African studies in verifying their discussion.

Another book, Barboza's *Door of No Return: The Legend of Gorée Island* (1994), also focuses on West Africa. Author Stephen Barboza spent many months in Africa, searching for his own West African roots and researching the history of Gorée Island. Located off the coast of Dakar, Senegal, the island today is a tourist and resort area but historically was a pivotal location for the slave trade. The author notes that the island "served as a doorway. Europeans used this 'doorway' as an entry point to the mainland, about two miles away; Africans unwillingly used it as an exit from their homes. They were never to return" (p. 1). Today visitors can tour the dungeons in the House of Slaves and pass through the same doorway as did the Africans who were being taken as slaves. Barboza provides a history of the island from its volcanic formation to its initial role in the Portuguese slave trade, later role in the American slave trade, and life on the island today. The book is illustrated with color photographs taken by the author and others. Illustration credits, acknowledgments and an index are provided.

Informational books support all areas of the elementary curriculum and are one of the most important genres for learning about other countries. Teachers can read informational books aloud as many teachers do with *People* and can lead discussions that focus on the colorful photographs in books such as those noting cultural details in *Carnaval*. Students can consult informational books when they are engaged in inquiry projects on science, social studies, and thematic topics and concepts. They can also turn to an informational book to whet their curiosity about personal topics of interest. The unique formats of informational books such as the counting framework, ABC concept books, and photo-essays serve as exemplary models for students' own writing. As the informational genre continues to gain in popularity, an increased number of books with a global perspective should become available.

Biography

Biography as a genre can trace its roots to ancient storytellers who recounted the lives of epic heroes such as Odysseus, Gilgamesh, and King Arthur. However, as a genre within global children's literature, biography is underrepresented. The genre does not even warrant an entry in the 1996 *International Companion Encyclopedia of Children's Literature*, edited by Peter Hunt and Sheila Ray. A paucity of biographies written in other countries is available in the United States. Most of those distributed in the United States are Holocaust memoirs. Domestic books about international figures have traditionally been limited in scope and of mixed literary quality. They have focused primarily on Western European explorers, artists, and historical figures. Individuals from Asia, Africa, or South America have received little attention. The few autobiographies available for children are written by British authors of children's books.

As with informational books, many U.S. publishers support biography series that feature international personalities. For example, the "Tell Me About" series of Carolrhoda books for grades K–3 includes biographies of artists such as Malam's

Vincent Van Gogh (1998). Franklin Watts has two biography series for students in grades 4 to 6, "Ancient Biographies," which includes a book about *Tutankhamum* by Green (1996) and "Monarchs," which includes books about British rulers.

Originally published in England, the Oxford University Press series "What's Your Story?" features easy-to-read biographies in a 32-page format on individuals such as Langley's *Hans Christian Andersen* (1998) and Grant's *Eric the Red* (1997). As part of the series, Pratima Mitchell has written an informative biography about *Gandhi: The Father of Modern India* (1997), which documents Gandhi's life from his birth in 1869 to his assassination shortly after India's independence in 1947. As Mitchell writes, "He had given people all over the world a new way of dealing with anger and hatred—the way of truth, nonviolence, and love for the enemy" (p. 31). The biography includes a list of "Difficult words used in this story" and an index. Mrinal Mitra's watercolor illustrations are detailed, realistic, and effectively support the text.

Noted American biographer for children Russell Freedman shares the life of Frenchman Louis Braille in *Out of Darkness: The Story of Louis Braille* (1997). This complete biography recounts the life of the inspirational man who invented the Braille system of written language for the blind. Freedman's relatively short book of 79 pages can be read independently by children in grades 3 to 5. It is illustrated with pencil drawings by Kate Kiesler and diagrams of the Braille alphabet. Louis lost his sight in an accident when he was 3-years-old and received a scholarship to attend the Royal Institute for Blind Youth in Paris. While studying there, young Louis determined to develop an easier system to enable blind people to read and write, his raised-dot alphabet. Freedman notes that "in his short lifetime, Louis Braille had done more than anyone in history to bring blind people into the mainstream of life" (p. 76).

Canadian writer and editor Hugh Brewster consulted primary sources to document the life of Anastasia, youngest daughter of Tsar Nicholas II. First published in Canada, *Anastasia's Album: The Last Tsar's Youngest Daughter Tells Her Own Story* (1996) is illustrated with archival photographs taken by Anastasia herself, Peter Christopher's contemporary color photographs, excerpts from Anastasia's album pages, and quotes from her letters. This photo-essay biography follows Anastasia's life from her birth in 1901 to the mysteries surrounding her death. Because her skeletal remains have never been found, no one knows for certain if she died with her family when they were executed in the cellar of a house in 1918. Anastasia's daily life is set against the backdrop of the political situation in Russia that led to revolution.

Ellen Levine has written a meticulously researched biography of *Anna Pavlova: Genius of the Dance* (1995). The Russian-born Pavlova, perhaps the world's greatest ballerina, brought the magic of ballet to audiences around the world. As Levine notes in the book's preface, "Before Anna Pavlova left her home in Russia in 1910 and traveled abroad, scarcely anyone in the United States had seen a ballet performance." Levine describes the highlights of Pavlova's life from her 1881 birth in St. Petersburg to her death in 1931. She carefully documents not only Pavlova's career development but also gives readers insights into Pavlova as a person. Several pages of black and white photographs are inserted into the center of the book.

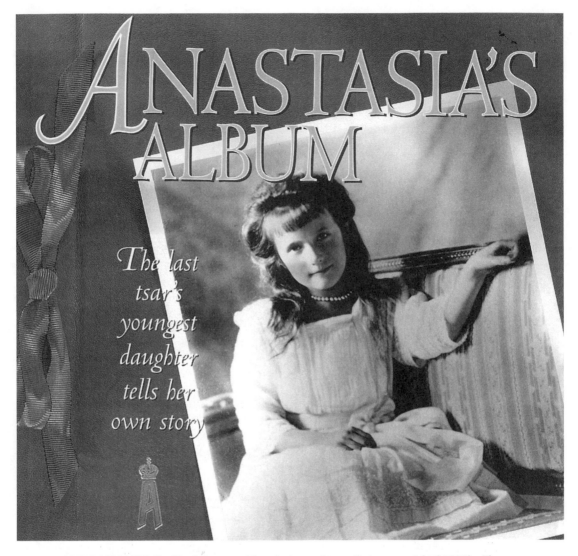

From ANASTASIA'S ALBUM by Hugh Brewster. Text, design and compilation copyright © 1996 by The Madison Press Limited. Color photograph copyright © 1996 Peter Christopher. Reprinted by permission of Hyperion Books for Children.

A glossary of ballet-related terms, an annotated bibliography of sources, and an index are included.

The picture-book biography has become a popular format in recent years; however, it is not limited to audiences of primary-grade children. In fact, many of the picture book biographies are more appropriate for children in the middle and upper elementary grades. A fine example of this format is *Sundiata, Lion King of Mali* (1992) by American author and artist David Wisniewski, who is well known for his award-winning cut-paper illustrations. Wisniewski based his book on the retelling of Sundiata's life by a Malinke griot and uses the storytelling format as a framework to describe Sundiata's experiences. This thirteenth-century ruler of Mali overcame physical disability and exile and returned victorious to save his country from invasion, leading it for "many golden years." The colorful cut-paper illustrations were carefully researched to authentically represent the Malinke culture. An author's note provides additional historical background and explains the author's research to create the text and illustrations.

In *Passage to Freedom: The Sugihara Story* (1997), Ken Mochizuki portrays the courageous story of the Japanese diplomat posted in Lithuania who saved thousands of Polish Jews from Nazi persecution. This picture-book biography is told in the first person from the perspective of Sugihara's son, who was 5 years old in 1940. Defying orders from the Japanese government, Chiune Sugihara issued Polish Jewish refugees visas to enter Japan. An afterword by Sugihara's son provides additional information, including the selection of his father to receive the "Righteous Among Nations" Award from Yad Vashem in Israel. The book's sepia-toned, scratchboard and mixed-media illustrations capture the story's mood. Each double-page spread positions text on the left-hand side and Dom Lee's full-page, realistic illustrations on the right.

Floyd Cooper tells the life of *Mandela: From the Life of the South African Statesman* (1996) in pictures and text. Beginning with Mandela's birth to a Thembu village chief who told Nelson to "always stand firm for what he believed was fair and right," the book chronicles Mandela's education far from home and events leading to his leadership of the African National Congress. It also discusses his 27-year imprisonment, his release in 1990, and his election as president of South Africa. Illustrations created with an oil wash in earth tones completely cover each double-page spread and enhance the setting and tone of the book. An author's note provides additional information; a pronunciation key and bibliography are also included.

The famous Egyptian queen is the subject of a picture book biography for older readers, *Cleopatra* (1994), a collaboration by American authors Diane Stanley and Peter Vennema. Many myths and misinformation surround Cleopatra's life. As the authors point out in the "Note on Ancient Sources," "everything we know about Cleopatra was written by her enemies." Although she was queen during Roman times, Cleopatra was not Egyptian but of Macedonian Greek ancestry. She is known for her remarkable beauty and intelligence. This biography describes her relationships with Caesar and Mark Antony and the mysteries surrounding her downfall and loss of her empire to Octavian. Lavishly illustrated and formatted, the book captures the Egyptian setting and culture with Stanley's realistic gouache paintings in vivid colors. The text is printed on a background of painted mosiac tiles surrounded by a mosaic tile border. The book includes an epilogue, pronunciation guide, and bibliography.

Autobiographies and memoirs are also written for children. These two closely related genres are often difficult to distinguish. Hancock (2000) points out that in an autobiography, the author "reflects on the true details of . . . one's own life" while a memoir is "a record of events based on the writer's own observation . . . often a retrospective account that focuses on a memorable or tragic event in the author's life" (p. 148). Very few autobiographies with an international focus exist for children, and the subjects are limited to British authors of children's books. Two beloved British authors, now deceased, wrote autobiographies; for example, Edith Nesbit's *Long Ago When I Was Young* (1987) and Roald Dahl's *Boy* (1984). Contemporary British author-illustrator Michael Foreman shares his life in words and pictures in a two-volume autobiography, *War Boy* (1989) and *After the War Was Over* (1995).

The memoir has become an increasingly popular genre for children. These books are appropriate for children in the upper elementary and middle school grades. Early memoirs with an international focus include Newbery Honor Books *The Upstairs Room* by Johanna Reiss (1972) and *Upon the Head of the Goat: A Childhood in Hungary, 1939–1944* (1981) by Aranka Siegel, both of which recount the authors' childhoods during World War II. Recently published memoirs represent a range of cultures and perspectives.

Vedat Dalokay, the former mayor of Ankara, Turkey, recalls his relationship with a special old woman in *Sister Shako and Kolo the Goat: Memories of My Childhood in Turkey*, published in Turkey in 1979 and translated into English in 1994. This memoir provides a loving tribute to Sister Shako, who, after her husband and two sons were killed in the "vendetta," moves with her goats to the author's village, where she lives in a hut by the river. As a young boy, Dalokay befriends the woman and becomes attached to her and her goat, Kolo, who soon bears kids. The book, organized as a series of short vignettes, describes specific events or experiences shared by the author and Sister Shako and provides insights into village life. Footnotes contain additional explanation about specific aspects of Turkish language and culture. The translator, Güner Ener, gives additional background about the book and its translation in an endnote. Sister Shako's special qualities and the loving intergenerational relationship that develops between her and the young boy create a beautiful tribute to the memory of Sister Shako and the author, who has since passed away.

Alma Flor Ada's (1998) memoir, *Under the Royal Palms: A Childhood in Cuba* is a collection of reminiscences from childhood in prerevolutionary Cuba, rather than a single, connected life narrative. In these stories, Ada recounts individuals from her past who helped to shape the adult she became, many of whom were relatives who lived together in a large, old house called *La Quinta Simoni*. Readers meet her grandmother, cousins, parents, uncles, and aunts, a ballet teacher named Gilda, and Madame Marie, a Jewish woman who escaped Nazi persecution in occupied France. Numerous black and white photographs help readers to visualize the people and settings in Ada's stories. The author's introduction and epilogue speak directly to her readers, providing additional context and drawing them into her experiences. She also invites children to look for and share their life stories, as she has done in this heartwarming volume. Most appropriate for middle grade readers, this collection may appeal to a slightly older audience than do the majority of Ada's books—picture books and folktale retellings—but children should enjoy learning more about an author whom they already know from earlier encounters with her works. Certainly, adults can read aloud selections from this book with younger children engaged in an author study.

Water Buffalo Days: Growing Up in Vietnam (1997) provides a picture of author Huynh Quang Nhuong's childhood that revolved around the beloved family water buffalo. The story begins with the death of Water Jug, the old family water buffalo, which led to acquiring a new yearling bull calf. Six-year-old Nhuong quickly makes friends with the calf, helps his older cousin train the calf for riding, and explores the surrounding rice fields with him to catch field crabs. Eventually, fully grown to his giant size, the bull earns his name, Tank, after defeating the town herd's rival leader in a fateful battle. From that time on, Tank's responsibilities, in addition to work in the field, include protecting the herd from wild predators, such as crocodiles, wild hogs, or tigers. However, his legendary prowess cannot protect Tank from the spreading war, and one day a stray bullet from a nearby battle hits Tank, causing the loss of Nhuong's dearest companion and childhood innocence. Tank's sad death symbolizes the larger tragedy of a beautiful land nearly destroyed by fighting. The author himself was wounded in that war and now lives in the United States. His poignant story is sensitively illustrated by Jean and Mou-sien Tseng's black and white sketches that help readers to visualize Nhuong and Tank's playful shared adventures.

Set against China's Great Proletarian Cultural Revolution in 1966, *Red Scarf Girl: A Memoir of the Cultural Revolution* (1997) provides readers the perspective of Ji-li Jiang who was 12-years-old during this turbulent time in Chinese history. The unabridged book is also available on audiotape. Ji-li grew up in a close-knit, happy family—she was bright, popular with her classmates, and loyal to Chairman Mao. She proudly wore her "red scarf, the emblem of Young Pioneers" (p. 1). But the cultural revolution soon turned her world upside down and forced Ji-li to question her long-held beliefs. Because her grandfather had been a landlord, Ji-li's family was the victim of discrimination and abuse during the fearful Cultural Revolution. Ji-li's loyalties are repeatedly tested as family and friends suffer all kinds of persecution. An epilogue informs readers about the author's life after the book concludes, when she is 14 years old, and a lengthy glossary explains unfamiliar vocabulary.

Recent years have seen an increase in memoirs written by Holocaust survivors who were children during World War II. Many of these survivors are now grandparents who want others to know and remember their stories. Livia Bitton-Jackson shares the horror of her childhood in *I Have Lived a Thousand Years: Growing Up in the Holocaust* (1997). As 13-year-old Elli Friedman, she lived a relatively normal life revolving around boys, school, and family in Hungary. When the Nazis invaded in 1944, however, the Holocaust became a firsthand experience for her and the other Jews of Somorja as they were deported first to a ghetto in Hungary and eventually to Auschwitz. For 11 months (which seemed as endless as a thousand years), Elli, her mother, and brother managed to survive against terrifying odds: the daily struggle to stay alive and also several specific moments—including a selection in which Elli was separated from her mother and sent with a group headed for the gas chamber—when Elli miraculously was spared, usually because of her own courage, boundless determination, and quick thinking even when her mother lost hope. After the war, the trio—all that remained from a much larger extended family—returned to their hometown to discover that it no longer could be their home. Finally, in 1951 they emigrated to the United States. Today, as a grandmother who divides her time between the United States and Israel, Bitton-Jackson tells her story with the "hope that learning about past evils will help us avoid them in the future" (p. 11) and the simple, but profound, message she exemplified: "Never give up" (p. 11). Locations and dates for each chapter give mature readers a solid grounding for following the progression of Bitton-Jackson's early life. Two appendices of chronology further summarize important events for her family and the larger historical context; a glossary defines unfamiliar German, Hungarian, and Jewish terms and names.

Batchelder award–winning *Thanks to My Mother* (1998) by Schoschana Rabinovici describes the courageous efforts of a mother to keep her daughter alive during the Nazi persecution. Originally written in 1991 in Hebrew, this memoir was first translated into German and subsequently translated from German into English. A Lithuanian Jew, the author was born in 1932 as Susanne Weksler. When Germany occupied Vilnius in June, 1941, the lives of Lithuanian Jews would forever be changed. First they were forced to live in a ghetto, followed by many "actions" in which Jews were murdered. Eventually, they were transported to concentration camps. Throughout, Susanne's mother possessed a quick mind and strong determination to survive and to ensure her daughter's safety. As a child in the ghetto and camps, Susanne wrote poems that are included in the book. Her vivid images of the horrors that she and others experienced are told in terrifying detail. The book concludes: "Out of our entire family, only we three remained: My uncle, Wolodja; my mother, Raja; and I, Susie Weksler" (p. 246).

Noted children's author and illustrator Anita Lobel presents her personal childhood story in *No Pretty Pictures: A Child of War* (1998). Born to a middle-class Jewish family in Kraków, Poland, Anita was only 5 when the Germans invaded Poland. In order to escape being deported, she and her younger brother pretended to be their nanny's children and hid with her first in the Polish countryside and later in a Benedictine convent. After they were discovered, Anita and her brother were transported to Plaszów camp and then to Ravensbrück. After liberation, they were sent to Sweden to recover from tuberculosis. Miraculously Anita's parents both survived, and she and her brother were reunited with them. The family lived in Stockholm before emigrating to the United States when Anita was 16. The book includes black and white photographs of Anita and her family. She poignantly writes, "I am a grandmother now. That October afternoon in 1939 in Kraków, when I still had a grandmother, when I knew nothing of journeys in boxcars, I was five years old. I was ten years old when I climbed onto a boxcar transport . . . Mine is only another story" (p. 190).

By reading biographies, children meet real historical and contemporary people from around the globe. Children enjoy selecting a biography to read and sharing its subject with others. This sharing can take many forms: dressing up like the person and discussing that person's life in role; participating with a peer in a simulated interview; creating a visual display; or developing a power-point presentation. As children read biographies, they learn how they are crafted. Children can select a person from another part of the world or a family member or friend who was born outside the United States as the subject for a biography they will research and write. Biographies bring to life people whom young readers from any country may emulate, with whom they may identify, and from whom they may receive inspiration. Biographies help children realize the commonalities that bind all people together, as well as the unique historical and cultural circumstances that influence people's lives.

Poetry

Chapter 2 notes that one benefit of global poetry is children experiencing the rich variety of sound that is distinct to different languages and dialects. The rhythm, rhyme, and imagery that are so appealing to children in their native languages can provide children from other cultures with the flavor of diverse linguistic patterns. However, as noted in Chapter 3, poetry also presents special challenges to crossing borders precisely because its poetic expression is the most difficult form to translate from one language to another.

International poetry has been delighting young American audiences for centuries, as Mother Goose rhymes (found around the world) are part of the "foundation of a child's literary heritage" (Cullinan & Galda, 1998, p. 168) and children's introduction to poetry, in particular. Other early poetry available for children in the United States came mostly from British poets, including William Blake's tender *Songs of Innocence* (1789). Edward Lear popularized the limerick form of nonsense poetry with his *The Book of Nonsense* (1846), and Lewis Carroll's nonsense poems, such as *The Walrus and the Carpenter* (1986), were included in *Alice's Adventures in Wonderland* (1865) and *Through the Looking Glass* (1871). Scottish poet Robert Louis Stevenson's classic collection, *A Child's Garden of Verses* (1885), was well-loved on both sides of the Atlantic. A. A. Milne's delightful verse captured the child's world in *When We Were Very Young* (1924) and *Now We Are Six* (1927). English poet Eleanor Farjeon received the first Hans Christian Andersen Award in 1956, and a British award named for her is bestowed annually for "distinguished services to children's books" (Sutherland & Arbuthnot, 1991, p. 317). One of the few translated works of poetry for children cited by Meigs, Eaton, Nesbitt, and Viguers (1969), Heinrich Hoffman's *Struwwelpeter (Slovenly Peter)*, came out of Germany in about 1844. Huck, Hepler, Hickman, and Kiefer (1997) consider these hilariously dire warnings about bad behavior to be forerunners for similar slapstick modern verse by American poets Shel Silverstein and Jack Prelutsky. The Japanese haiku form is widely known and imitated today in the United States, and the verse of Japanese poet Michio Mado, 1994 recipient of the Hans Christian Andersen Award, has been available to American audiences since 1992 in *The Animals*.

In spite of the difficulties with poetry translation and the underrepresentation of poetry in global children's literature, noteworthy recent examples present at least three trends worth examining: poetic and playful uses of language, poetic forms (both unique to a culture and universal), and images of life from countries around the world.

Poetic Language

Poetry should satisfy children's "natural response to rhythm" (Huck, Hepler, Hickman, & Kiefer, 1997, p. 393). It intrigues children with sounds, such as rhyme, repetition, and nonsense words or onomatopoeia. It stimulates children's imaginations with figurative language. International poetry can even introduce children to other languages and English dialects.

Grace Nichols, born in Guyana and now living in Britain, uses lilting rhyme and strong rhythm in *Asana and the Animals: A Book of Pet Poems* (1997). This collection portrays a young girl's fascination with animals, both real and imaginary, such as cats, parrots, caterpillars, alligators, and jogging ocelots. The poem, "Things I Like in the Sea That Go By Swimmingly," begins with a definite rhyming beat, while repetition adds emphasis to the rhyme and rhythm of "Grasshopper One" and internal rhyme and onomatopoeia add pleasure in "Pit-a-Pat-a-Parrot." Sarah Adams's bold illustrations are warm-colored linocuts with oil-based inks in gold tones. The lack of black lines helps to evoke the summery, tropical-hazy mood of many of the rhymes.

Onomatopoeia and animal sounds contribute to the poetic language of *Hush: A Thai Lullaby* by Minfong Ho (1996a). This gentle, rhythmic verse portrays evening sounds and a mother's attempts to quiet all the surrounding animals—mosquito, lizard, cat, mouse, frog, pig, duck, monkey, water buffalo, and elephant—so her baby can sleep. Finally, peace reigns and Mother sleeps, but Baby is wide awake. Ho, who now lives in the United States, composed this lullaby for *her* child while living in her native Thailand. Holly Meade's cut-paper collage and ink illustrations were inspired by Thai art forms. These Caldecott Honor pictures include basket-weave and corrugated cardboard textures and fabric prints that complement the village setting.

The Magic Pocket (1998) is a companion volume to Michio Mado's *The Animals*. The Empress Michiko of Japan translated the 14 poems, and each two-page spread contains the Japanese version on the left side and the English translation on the right. Thus readers in the United States can see how each poem looks written in Japanese characters. Nearly every poem features repetition, "Fingers" are personified in the poem by that name, and "Song of an Umbrella" (comparing it to a flower that opens and shuts) presents a good example of metaphor. Topics of other poems, like these, are appealing to children's interests. For example, "Hermit Crab" captures a childlike perspective regarding the house address for this small creature. 1984 Hans Christian Andersen award–winning illustrator Mitsumasa Anno created the delicate, hand-painted monotone paper collage decorations for each poem. Spare layout with generous white space bordered by buff page edges make this a handsome volume.

Most of the poems in Naomi Shihab Nye's extensive anthology, *The Tree Is Older Than You Are: A Bilingual Gathering of Poems & Stories from Mexico with Paintings by Mexican Artists* (1995), are parallel Spanish and English versions. In addition to the poems, 24 full-color paintings and some folktales are included. A few Mayan selections, such as "Prayer to the Corn in the Field," come from Tzeltal, which is first translated into Spanish and retains a lovely poetic rhythm and repetition. "Boats" provides a fine example of figurative language that captures the universal essence of poetry by comparing it to a folded paper boat into which life fits. The end matter contains "Notes on the Contributors" with information about the writers and artists whose work is included, "A Note on the Folktales," "A Note on the Translations and Translators," and "Acknowledgments," with information about the sources of the paintings and copyrights for the written selections. Three indices and a list of illustrations conclude this remarkable volume.

My Mexico/México mío (1996) is a bilingual collection of 18 poems by Tony Johnston, a former 15-year Mexican resident. In these selections she celebrates images of everyday life, which F. John Sierra, a Mexican American, impressionistically illustrates with color pencils over watercolor and airbrushed backgrounds. The resulting soft but richly hued pictures evoke the land and people of Mexico and complement the poems, for example, the characterization of "Houses" as "a bouquet of flowers" (p. 4). The figurative language of this poem is typical of others, such as "Street Dogs," which compares roaming dogs to "papers blown" (p. 15). Several poems personify objects, such as walls, adobe bricks, and the city; others, such as "Downtown, Mexico City," present a sobering view of a homeless mother and child. A glossary at the end includes pronunciations and meanings for Spanish words used in the English versions.

Two books celebrate Caribbean dialects by employing the vernaculars' natural lilt. Australian Frané Lessac, a Caribbean resident for many years, pairs her brilliant oil, watercolor, and gouache paintings with West Indian proverbs and poems in *Caribbean Canvas* (1987), published in the United States in 1994. Una Marson's "Kinky Hair Blues" (accompanied by an oil painting titled "Disco"), "Jamaican Alphabet" by Louise Bennett, and Susan J. Wallace's "Ilan' Life" demonstrate especially well the poetic rhythm of the local language.

Likewise, Jamaican-born Valerie Bloom's *Fruits: A Caribbean Counting Poem* (1997) portrays the playful rivalry between two sisters in the poet's native dialect. As the older sister counts their favorite fruits, she usually devises a clever way to keep most for herself. All the fruits are tropical and are a good way to introduce American readers to some less familiar ones, such as guinep, guava, sweet-sop, June-plum, naseberry, and jackfruit. A glossary explains some terms, and the spelling in text reflects Jamaican Patwa sounds, such as *smaddy* for *somebody*. David Axtell's oil paintings show their canvas texture through bright colors as luscious as the fruits depicted.

Poetic Forms

The form of a poem should suit its meaning, and children should develop appreciation for poetry's diverse structures (Huck, Hepler, Hickman, & Kiefer, 1997). Children may expect all poetry to rhyme and be structured in typical stanzas, but experience with various poetic forms can help them to broaden their understanding for structures ranging from lyrical poetry to free verse.

Jane Yolen's edited collection of *Street Rhymes Around the World* (1992) uses this well-known form to compile verses universally created and performed by children in their everyday play. For example, a hand-waving game rhyme comes from India, a jump rope chant from China, and a hide-and-seek rhyme from Zambia. The 32 chants exemplify both our human universality and cultural uniqueness. Each rhyme translated into English is paired with its bilingual version, and when those languages use non-Roman alphabets or characters, the bilingual version is a transliteration, or phonetic translation, of the original. In addition to India, China, and Zambia, countries represented include Brazil, Israel, Japan, Russia, Mexico, England, Greece, Germany, Denmark, France, Armenia, the Netherlands, and the United States. A native from each country illustrates the accompanying rhyme, thus introducing international artists who may be new to American audiences.

From: FRUITS: A Caribbean Counting Poem by Valerie Bloom, illustrations by Dave Axtell. Jacket illustration copyright, © 1996 by Dave Axtell. Reprinted by permission of Henry Holt and Company, LLC

In *A Caribbean Counting Book,* Faustin Charles (1996) from Trinidad and now a British resident has compiled rhymes with the familiar counting structure of many children's games and songs. This unique book includes not only rhymes from English dialects, but also ones translated from Spanish, Dutch, and French, reflecting the multilingual, multicultural character of the Caribbean islands. Several poems also show the close similarity of these rhymes to ones well-known to American audiences, such as "One-two, Buckle My Shoe" or "Ten Little Monkeys." Roberta Arenson's luminous collages depict appropriate tropical colors and match the verses' playful mood.

John Agard and Grace Nichols's collection *No Hickory No Dickory No Dock: Caribbean Nursery Rhymes* (1995) demonstrates the universality of Mother Goose. The authors, both born in Guyana and now living in England, include original compositions and ones remembered from their childhoods. They even give a playful twist to old European favorites, such as the title verse in which the mouse protests his innocence. Others, such as "One Two Anancy," show their African roots. This union of Caribbean, English, and African roots creates a special international feeling in one book. American Cynthia Jabar's scratchboard illustrations with rich colors outlined in black make the rhymes dance visually. Endpaper illustrations depict a map of the Caribbean area, on which to locate the settings for these rhymes.

Next, a pair of collections profile two Japanese haiku poets. Dawnine Spivak's *Grass Sandals: The Travels of Basho* (1997) tells the story of a much-loved poet who lived and traveled throughout Japan in the seventeenth century. Basho set an example of simplicity as he chronicled details about his daily experiences and of nature. The quiet narrative accompanies samples of Basho's haiku and a Japanese character (with its transliteration and English translation) symbolizing an idea from each poem. A preface to the main text explains the haiku form and Japanese written characters. End matter provides a map of places Basho visited, a list of what he saw, and brief biographical information about Basho. Demi's signature illustrations, rendered in colored ink with Oriental brushes on textured paper, are perfect complements for this sensitive, tender account. The endpapers show Japanese writing and depict Basho writing a poem on a banana leaf for on-looking deer. Rich colors within delicate shapes echo the book's themes.

Matthew Gollub's *Cool Melons—Turn to Frogs!: The Life and Poems of Issa* (1998), who lived and worked in eighteeth-century Japan, recounts the life and work of another Japanese poet. This story, more traditionally biographical than that of Basho, chronicles Issa's unhappy childhood after his mother's death and father's remarriage to a jealous stepmother. At age 14, Issa (actually named Kobayashi Yataro) was banished from home and went to live in Edo (Tokyo), where he worked for and trained with a master poet. Eventually, like Basho, Issa became a pilgrim journeying around his country on foot and recording his observations of nature and life in haiku verses. He spent the last years of his life back in his home village, where he finished composing his more than 20,000 haiku. Samples of his poems intersperse the story of his life. Each verse is depicted in its Japanese characters along the pages' outside borders, and Kazuko G. Stone, a Japanese-born American resident, captures scenes from Issa's life and illustrates the haiku in her watercolor paintings. Background notes about the book's creation, selected poems, the translations, and haiku comprise the end matter. Gollub explains that he attempted to interpret the poems in his translations, rather than strictly follow the haiku syllable count. Notes about haiku enlighten readers about this art form, and information about the author and illustrator's collaborative research for this book is helpful.

Images of Life

The content of poetry should be relevant to children's lives and should help them gain new insights about life (Huck, Hepler, Hickman, & Kiefer, 1997). International poetry that presents "slices of life" from around the world provides vicarious experiences, just as all poetry "invites participation in that experience" (McClure, 1990, p. 35) and broadens children's ability to relate to other cultures. Hopkins (1987) states, "No matter where and when poets live, or where and when they write poetry, all write of everyday happenings from their own points of view about their environments" (p. 9). Canadian author Jean Little exemplifies this in her collection of the fictional Kate Bloomfield's poems and vignettes about life, *Hey World, Here I Am!* (1986), as wryly shown in "Today," which captures the rebellious feelings children everywhere experience occasionally. Thus, young readers can realize how the world of childhood is both unique and universal.

In another of her outstanding creations, Palestinian American Naomi Shihab Nye has selected entries from 19 countries for her anthology, *The Space Between Our Footsteps: Poems and Paintings from the Middle East* (1998). More than 100 writers and artists represent the region's diversity from Morocco in northwestern Africa to Turkey in the north and Iran in the east. In addition, the collection includes Israeli, as well as Arab, voices. Each painting and poem is identified by its creator and translator, with biographical "Notes on the Contributors" provided in the end matter. As expected from a region too often troubled by war and conflict, many poems present sobering images of lives torn by strife. For example, Ronny Someck, an Iraqi-born Israeli immigrant, describes the bleak life in a refugee camp in "Poverty Line." However, other poems, for example, "Class Pictures" by Israeli Shlomit Cohen-Assif, present scenes that children from many cultures will recognize, such as the familiar appearance of classmates, and Lebanese-born poet Kaissar Afif captures the peaceful power of poetry to span cultures in "The Bridge." A list of acknowledgments, indexes to the poets, artists, and poems, and a list of illustrations complete this volume. Nye's introduction presents a fascinating personal account of her background and motivation for developing this anthology.

Maples in the Mist: Children's Poems from the Tang Dynasty, translated by Minfong Ho (1996b), a Chinese American born in Burma (now known as Myanmar), demonstrates that poetry written more than 1,000 years ago can be relevant to contemporary children's lives. Ho grew up chanting these poems and decided to translate them for her own children's benefit and appreciation of their heritage, as explained in "A Note from the Translator." Gems, such as "Moon" by Li Bai, capture a child's wonder and imagination about night. Another, "On the Pond" by Bai Ju-Yi, presents such universal childhood antics as picking forbidden flowers. Versions of the poems in Chinese characters border the page edges outside the traditional-style, soft watercolor illustrations by Jean and Mou-Sien Tseng, both Taiwan-born U.S. residents. Biographical notes about the poets conclude this collection.

Two works by Monica Gunning return readers to the Jamaica of her childhood. The earlier *Not a Copper Penny in Me House: Poems from the Caribbean* (1993) is illustrated with Frané Lessac's full-color gouache paintings and offers an intimate view of island life, as in "Roadside Peddlers" who hawk their wares and in "Classes Under the Trees" which depicts school life. Other poems remember Christmas and the John Canoe dancers, the "Corner Shop" where groceries can be bought on credit during hard times, washing clothes in the river, a hurricane, shining shoes with a red hibiscus, and riding the market bus to Kingston.

Gunning's companion volume, *Under the Breadfruit Tree: Island Poems* (1998), provides more insiders' perspectives, as in her Grandma's grateful words about the "manna" of the breadfruit tree (p. 7). Many of the verses in this book vividly describe friends and relatives, such as "Hilda, the Higgler," "Mean Old Aunt Maggie," and the vain "Uncle Rufus." A series of seven poems celebrates the life and death of her best friend Connie. Simple black and white scratchboard illustrations by Fabricio Venden Broeck of Mexico decorate the pages, and a glossary explains unfamiliar Jamaican terms.

Finally, Isaac Olaleye shares his childhood memories of growing up in a rain forest village in *The Distant Talking Drum: Poems from Nigeria* (1995). A poem reminiscent of Gunning's "Classes Under the Trees" mentioned earlier, "In the Ebony Room," describes school lessons interrupted by a sudden rainstorm. In this culture, too, laundry is done in the stream, the village tales-teller regales children with stories "about Ijapa, the treacherous tortoise" (p. 10), a stone for grinding black-eyed peas and melon seeds is the symbolic "heart of the hut" (p. 16), children play hide-and-seek in the dark, and the village market is a feast for the senses. Frané Lessac's distinctive, brightly colored, gouache paintings with traditional African border designs exude tropical images to accompany the poetic "drum beat."

Poetry collections such as those described in this section have the potential to evoke vicarious experiences that cross international boundaries. On the one hand, their inclusion of languages or dialects from diverse cultures, their use of poetic forms—such as haiku—particularly associated with a country, and their portrayal of life in specific settings help readers to broaden their acquaintance with unique cultures. On the other hand, poetry everywhere employs rhythm, repetition, rhyme, figurative language, and other devices, nursery and game rhyme forms, and images of life that demonstrate the universality of childhood and humankind. Teachers can incorporate poetry such as this on a daily basis by reading it aloud to demonstrate the beauty of poetic language, to broaden children's appreciation for diverse poetic forms, and to provide highly condensed glimpses of life with which children can both identify and expand their horizons. Despite its special challenges for transcending borders, poetry is a vital component of global children's literature.

Folklore

Long ago in a distant land, people nestled around a campfire and listened to a storyteller enthrall them with the adventures of "little people," the legends of heroes, or the humorous antics of animal tricksters. Thus, folklore as we know it today was born—the body of traditional literature that has no known author but rather has been passed down from generation to generation through oral storytelling. Then, at some point in time, someone wrote down the tale so it could be shared through the written word and disseminated beyond the boundaries of its creators. Lukens (1999) points out, "Because of scholarly collecting, folktales that once flourished only in communities where people did not read or write have become the property of all people" (p. 25). The folklore genre is vast and, in terms of global literature, probably the most widely read and known to American children. In children's literature, this genre includes folk and fairy tales, fables, myths, legends, and epics.

Folklore as a genre specifically published for children probably can trace its origin to the British collectors Andrew Lang and Joseph Jacobs. Between 1889 with the publication of *The Blue Fairy Book* until 1910 with the publication of the *The Lilac Fairy Book*, Lang edited 12 collections of folk and fairy tales from around the world for children. Each volume is designated by a color and has been reissued multiple times. Similarly Joseph Jacobs collected and retold folklore for children in volumes such as *English Fairy Tales* (1890) and *Celtic Fairy Tales* (1892). In 1925 Charles Finger received the Newbery Medal for *Tales from the Silver Lands* (1924), a collection of stories he had collected from South American Indians. Generally, American children are most familiar with the folklore of Europe and retellings by Charles Perrault and brothers Jacob and Wilhelm Grimm of such favorites as "Cinderella," "Little Red Riding Hood," and "Rumpelstiltskin."

Much research has been conducted by folklore scholars regarding the origins of tales, different classification systems of folktales, and theories to explain the similarity of folktales across cultures. For example, the Cinderella variant appears to exist in most cultures around the world. Many cultures have animal trickster tales such as the spider Anansi of West Africa, the raven of the Inuits, and Br'er Rabbit of southern African Americans.

Although folk literature is very popular and much enjoyed by children, several issues must be considered when selecting folklore to share in classrooms. Readers must be aware of and sensitive to the origin of the tale as well as the issue of authenticity in the retelling of the tale. Some believe that only members of a given culture should be retelling their tales. This issue is further complicated if the tale is from a non-English speaking culture. Then, in addition to preserving an authentic retelling, the tale must also be translated into English. Further, to retell a folktale so it can be shared with children, authors must make adaptations to the original source. Bosma (1992) points out that "each type of adaptation must be evaluated on the basis of how accurately the retelling reflects the oral storytelling tradition, how authentically the culture of the people is preserved, and how carefully the essence of the tale has been maintained" (p. 6). When selecting retellings to share with children, we should check to see if information about the original source or sources is identified to ensure the authenticity of the retelling and the background of the author that qualifies him or her to retell the tale.

Folklore for children is usually presented either in collections such as *Señor Cat's Romance and Other Favorite Stories from Latin America* by González (1997) or as individual stories presented in many of the books discussed in this section. Often individual stories are published in picture book format with illustrations conveying visual representations about the culture of the tale. Because of the large body of folklore currently available for children, this section will focus on recently published titles primarily from cultures underrepresented in folklore for children. Books will be grouped by cultures and regions of the world.

Maori of New Zealand

Two native New Zealanders of Maori ancestry bring young readers traditional tales from the Maori. Noted opera singer Dame Kiri Te Kanawa wrote *Land of the Long White Cloud: Maori Myths, Tales and Legends* (1989). In the preface she explains, "The stories in this book are purely my recollection of those tales that I remembered and loved best when I was a child. Like all good stories they have probably changed in the telling and I am sure there are as many versions of the tales as there are tellers" (p. 9). Originally published in Great Britain, the book is a collection of trickster tales about Maui, creation stories, and tribal legends. Dame Kanawa includes the tale, "Maui Tames the Sun" which is also retold by Gavin Bishop as an individual tale described in the following paragraph. Magnificent, colorful paintings by award-winning British illustrator Michael Foreman accompany each tale. A glossary of terms is provided.

Maui, the trickster, is the subject of Gavin Bishop's retelling, *Maui and the Sun* (1996). This tale explains how we came to have "light both night and day." Maui and his brother want the sun to stay in the sky longer to extend daylight. So Maui devises a plan to capture the sun and keep it shining in the sky. When the sun tries to trick Maui by setting, Maui ensures light by pulling "the moon from out of the sea." The author's pen-and-ink and watercolor illustrations extend across both pages of each spread to enhance the text.

Africa

The diverse cultures of Africa have a long and rich tradition of oral storytelling. West African griots "kept official histories. Some of the recitations could take twelve days" (Temple, Martinez, Yokota & Naylor, 1998, p. 160).

The Ethiopian tale retold by Kurtz, *Fire on the Mountain* (1994), tells how Alemayu, a young shepherd boy, outsmarts a wealthy, boastful man to gain money for himself and his sister. The author grew up in Ethiopia and heard this tale as a child. She includes an author's note with additional information about the tale. When his parents die, Alemayu leaves the "beautiful mountains" to find his sister, who works as a cook for a wealthy man. Alemayu tends the man's cows and claims that he can stay "in the cold air of the mountains throughout the night with only a thick cloak against the cold." In disbelief, the man says he will reward the boy if he is successful; if he fails, Alemayu and his sister must leave. When the boastful man refuses to acknowledge the boy's success, he and his sister devise a clever plan to attain what the boy earned. American illustrator E. B. Lewis's watercolor illustrations portray the characters and the Ethiopian village setting.

Born in Mali, Baba Wagué Diakité retells and illustrates the West African tale, *The Hatseller and the Monkeys* (1999). American children will recognize the similarity between this traditional tale and the popular picture book by Slobodkina, *Caps for Sale* (1947). An author's note describes the origin of this West African story. In Diakité's retelling, BaMusa the hatseller travels to villages selling hats which he stacked on his head. One day he takes a nap under a shady mango tree in which monkeys are relishing the fruit. While BaMusa sleeps, the monkeys take the hats to wear and return to the tree. After eating mangoes himself, BaMusa devises a plan to recover his hats from the monkeys. Diakité painted the book's illustrations on ceramic tile. Each double-page spread is bordered with humorous poses of monkeys and conveys various elements of West African life.

Fioni Moodie shares the tale *Nabulela* (1996) from her hometown, North Nguni, South Africa. Originally published in Great Britain, this tale recounts how the village girls tricked the lake monster Nabulela out of his water home so the village men could slay him. Nabulela ate people and was feared by the villagers, who left him flat cakes to eat each evening. When a baby daughter, Nandi, is born to the chief, he spoils her, causing jealousy among the village girls. As punishment for the girls' attempts to kill Nandi, the chief tells them to bring back Nabulela's skin. The book ends happily, the girls are forgiven for their "wickedness," and the chief realizes he "did wrong always to favor my daughter." Moodie's detailed and colorful illustrations create the South African village setting.

Acclaimed American reteller of African folklore Verna Aardema shares the Ashanti tale, *Anansi Does the Impossible* (1997). In this well-known story, Anansi the Spider decides to buy "the tales our storytellers have told for generations" from the Sky God who owned them. The Sky God's price to return the stories to the earth people was steep: a live python, a real fairy, and 47 stinging hornets. Anansi, with his wife Aso's help, tricks the python, the fairy, and the hornets and presents them to the astonished Sky God. "And from that day to this, the folk stories of West Africa have been called Anansi Tales." Aardema's retelling is based on a 1930s British source and includes a glossary. This delightful tale is illustrated with brightly colored collages by Lisa Desimini, who fashioned the spiders from black velvet paper.

Eastern Europe

Two recent folktales originate from the Czech Republic. A retelling of the Czech legend, *Golem* by Wisniewski (1996), received the Caldecott Medal for its remarkable cut-paper illustrations. An author's note provides extensive background for this medieval Jewish tale about the giant of clay who would protect the Jews of Prague from oppression. With a "mighty spell" Rabbi Loew transformed the clay into a living giant, Golem. The Golem indeed protected the ghetto Jews; however, he killed and wounded many in the mob who tried to persecute the Jews. According to the legend, the emperor agreed to guarantee the Jews' safety if the rabbi would destroy Golem, so the rabbi performed another spell to turn Golem back to clay. The legend concludes that "since then, Golem has slept the dreamless sleep of clay. But many say he could awaken. Perhaps, when the desperate need for justice is united with holy purpose, Golem will come to life once more."

Czech artist Anna Vojtech collaborates with author Philmon Sturges to retell the traditional *Marushka and the Month Brothers* (1996), in which good triumphs over evil. The beautiful girl Marushka lives with her jealous stepmother and stepsister. Hoping to get rid of Marushka, the stepmother sends her out in a wintry day to get some violets. "She struggled up the mountain through the blinding snow. Far ahead she saw a light." Marushka comes to a hollow where the twelve Month Brothers live. They have the power to alter the seasons, and Brother March provides Marushka with violets. Twice more, Marushka's stepmother and stepsister send her out in the "bitter cold" to find strawberries, then apples. Each time one of the Month Brothers helps her. When the stepsister decides to venture out and find more apples, her rudeness toward Brother January causes a blizzard in which she and her mother perish. During each season, the Month Brothers continue to give Marushka violets, strawberries, and apples. Colorful paintings enhance the retelling, and wintry scenes extend across two wordless double-page spreads. Vojtech explains the background of the tale in an "artist's note."

The Caribbean

Two well-known Haitian folk characters, Bouki ("dummy" in Creole) and the trickster Malice, are featured in Wolkstein's *Bouki Dances the Kokioko: A Comical Tale from Haiti* (1997). Well-known American storyteller Wolkstein heard this tale at a storytelling night in Haiti in 1972 and retells it for children in this handsome volume with colorful illustrations by Jesse Sweetwater. The Haitian king loved to dance and created a dance and song called Kokioko. Without sufficient funds in the treasury to pay dancers to entertain him, the king devised a plan to reward 5,000 gourdes "to anyone who could dance the Kokioko." Because no one knew the dance, the king guaranteed himself wonderful entertainment each night for many months. One day, Malice, the king's gardener, happened upon the king singing and dancing the Kokioko and determined to receive the 5,000 gourdes. So he taught the dance to his friend Bouki, who successfully performed it for the king and received the gourdes, only to have them tricked away from him by Malice. The comical nature of the story is reinforced by Sweetwater's bright colorful paintings. A glossary of "Unfamiliar Words in Story" is provided.

Well-respected American folklorist Robert D. San Souci has collaborated with award-winning illustrator Brain Pinkney to retell *Cendrillon: A Caribbean Cinderella* (1998). As the author's note indicates, this version is based on the French Creole tale with the same name found in a nineteenth-century book. It follows the basic story line of Perrault's version with the addition of West Indian French Creole features such as field lizards being transformed into footmen and a "plump manicou" (opossum) becoming the coachman. A glossary defines French Creole words and phrases used throughout the tale. In this version, San Souci tells the story using the godmother as the narrator. Pinkney's colorful scratchboard illustrations create the Caribbean setting and completely cover both sides of each double-page spread.

South America

South America has a rich heritage of folklore. An amusing repetitive tale from Brazil, *So Say the Little Monkeys* (1998a), is retold by American author Nancy Van

Laan and illustrated by Korean-born Yumi Heo. The Indians who live along the Black River of Brazil told this story to explain why the "blackmouths" (tiny monkeys) do "not make any type of permanent home." Van Laan uses rhyme, sound words, and a rhythmic lilt to show why the monkeys procrastinated in building a house. Heo's pencil, oil, and collage illustrations contribute to the story's humor as they depict the monkeys' antics.

Nancy Van Laan has also collaborated with Argentinian Beatriz Vidal to bring readers two retellings: *The Legend of El Dorado* (1991), a Colombian tale, and *The Magic Bean Tree: A Legend from Argentina* (1998b). Vidal explains in "A Note About the Story" that she heard the legend of El Dorado, "the 'Gilded Man,' whose body was covered with gold dust" as a child in Argentina. In this story, the Chibcha Indians, who lived near Guatavita Lake, "holiest of all lakes," believed that a "mighty serpent slept beneath its surface, and that whoever touched the strange water and woke it would never return." The serpent casts a spell on the queen and young princess and lures them to the water, where they disappear. To honor the serpent and ensure the kingdom's security and the king's eventual reunion with his family, the people created a ritual of covering the king's body with gold dust. The king took his raft, laden with gold and emeralds, to the middle of the lake and cast these treasures into the water for the serpent. Each king has repeated this ritual and "to this day the treasures of El Dorado remain hidden." Vidal illustrates the legend with colorful, detailed paintings in shades of blues, greens, and browns.

In *The Magic Bean Tree*, a drought has come to the pampas, causing concern among the llama herders. A young Quechua boy, Topec, "decided that the rain had lost its way" and determines to find it. The magic carob tree tells Topec that the Great Bird of the Underworld is blocking the rain's way as it sleeps and its wings "reach from one end of the sky to the other." So Topec devises a plan to wake the bird and let the rain pour down. The story concludes, "Today the people of Argentina still tell the story of the brave Topec and the magic carob tree." Sources for the tale are listed and a glossary of unfamiliar words is provided. Vidal's folk-art style, gouache paintings add cultural details. The Great Bird, painted in hues of deep purple, extends across two pages and gives readers a sense of its power to block the rain.

Asia

The Cambodian story, *The Two Brothers* (1995) is retold by Minfong Ho, who was born in Burma, raised in Thailand, and worked in Cambodian refugee camps, and Cambodian-born and raised Saphon Ros. Both authors now live in the United States. In this tale, two brothers Kem and Sem live in a quiet Buddhist monastery. When they approach the abbot to tell him they want "to see the world outside," he consults his astrological charts and gives them each his blessings and advice. Kem follows the abbot's advice and becomes a wealthy merchant in China; Sem neglects to do as the abbot instructed, and hardship and bad luck befall him. Finally, he remembers and heeds the abbot's wise words and becomes "King of all Cambodia, just as the abbot of his quiet monastery had foreseen." Colorful illustrations by Jean and Mou-Sien Tseng are rich in cultural details and enhance the text.

Recipient of the Aesop Accolade of the American Folklore Society, Aaron Shephard retells, *The Crystal Heart: A Vietnamese Legend* (1998). In this story, Mi

Nuong, daughter of a mandarin, lives a sheltered life in her tower room. As she looks out her window one day, she sees a fishing boat and hears a man singing a beautiful tune. Captivated by this song, she waits to hear it again, and when she doesn't, Mi Nuong falls ill. The king sends a messenger to find the man, who is a poor fisherman. Although his song again touches the girl, when she sees the common fisherman, she rejects him with harsh words. Heartbroken, the man dies, and found on his chest is a large crystal that carried his spirit. When the crystal is brought to Mi Nuong, she realizes her cruelty and begs forgiveness. Joseph Daniel Fiedler's stunning paintings convey the haunting mood of the tale. Shepard has composed music and words for the fisherman's song, which is included in the end matter along with information about the story's source.

Award-winning author Laurence Yep retells *The Khan's Daughter: A Mongolian Folktale* (1997). The shepherd boy Möngke is told by his father that he will marry the Khan's daughter, so as a young man, Möngke sets forth to find the princess and declare his prophecy. To prove his worthiness, Möngke must pass three tests of his strength, bravery, and smartness. In the final test, the princess in disguise challenges him, Möngke proves successful, and marries the princess. This delightful tale portrays a clever girl and is adapted from a tale translated and published in 1868. Jean and Mou-Sien Tseng's watercolor illustrations, bordered by a frame, show fine details in the clothing, animals, and setting.

The Middle East

A Cinderella variant from Iraq, *The Golden Sandal: A Middle Eastern Cinderella Story* (1998) is retold by Rebecca Hickox and illustrated by Will Hillenbrand. In this version, Maha lives with her father, a fisherman, and her mean stepmother and stepsister. Magic resides in the red fish who transforms Maha so she can attend the merchant's celebration. Instead of a slipper, Maha loses a sandal, which is found by the merchant's son. The mixed-media illustrations fill both sides of each double-page spread and portray the Middle Eastern setting. The endmatter includes an author's note about the tale's origins and an illustrator's note about the artwork.

The oral tales of Scheherazade of Persia form the basis of many retellings. *The Rose's Smile: Farizad of the Arabian Nights* (1997), retold by David Kherdian, is less well-known than tales about Ali Baba or Aladdin. In this tale with a strong female heroine, Farizad is the sultan's daughter who has been taken from him and his wife at birth by her evil aunts. Both Farizad and her older brother, also kidnapped by the aunts, are raised by the Sultan's chief gardener. After the gardener and his wife die, an old woman tells Farizad that she must find three things to complete the garden: Bulbul al-Hazar, the Talking Bird; the Singing Tree; and the Water of Gold. Her courage saves not only her brother's life but also allows the secret of their births to be revealed so they are reunited with the Sultan and his wife. Italian-born Stefano Vitale has created magnificent, richly textured illustrations, and each page has a wide border in earthtones. Source notes for the tale are provided.

The study of folklore gives students insight into a culture's oral history and values. When folklore is studied in concert with historical and contemporary fiction, and informational material, students gain a fuller picture of the culture. Folklore lends itself to numerous learning experiences for children. They can become storytellers themselves, retelling individually or in pairs the tales they have read. Children enjoy dramatizing folklore through pantomime, role play, choral reading, or as a "play." In this section, two recent retellings of the Cinderella tale are discussed but countless others are available from cultures around the world. A comparative study of this tale or another popular motif such as trickster tales helps children become critical thinkers as they compare and contrast the tales. Many folktales are retold on audiotape by master storytellers that children will enjoy hearing, as further discussed in Chapter 5.

This chapter has highlighted current trends in international children's literature as they are represented in many genres: picture books, fiction, informational books, biography, poetry, and folklore. The chart, "Themes to Explore Across Genres," identifies some themes that connect books across genres discussed in this chapter. Children's understanding of a theme can be both broadened and deepened by reading books from various genres, and teachers may find the connections depicted in this chart a good starting point for planning how to share these books with children. In addition, when teachers read international children's books themselves, their own cultural knowledge and literary appreciation are enhanced. In turn, teachers can share these books with children as the tenth principle of the Convention of the Rights of the Child is realized, "You should be taught peace, understanding, tolerance and friendship among all people."

Themes to Explore across Genres

Problem-Solving

O Christmas Tree
Saturday Sancocho
Jamela's Dress
Yanomami
A Girl Named Disaster
Fire on the Mountain
Bouki Dances the Kokioko
The Magic Bean Tree

Overcoming Obstacles

Out of the Darkness: The Story of Louis Braille
Sundiata
Mandela
Red Scarf Girl
Cool Melons—Turn to Frogs!
Marushka and the Month Brothers
Harry Potter
The Muffin Child

Meeting the Challenge

One Night: A Story from the Desert
Jump Up Time
Learning to Swim in Swaziland
Nabulela
The Khan's Daughter
Flour Babies

Friendship

Henry & Horace
Cat and Mouse
Look Out, Cinder!
The Storyteller's Beads
Habibi
If You Could Be My Friend
Sister Shako and Kolo the Goat
Water Buffalo Days
Under the Breadfruit Tree
Stones in Water

CHAPTER

5 Sharing International Books across the Curriculum

A fourth-grade teacher in Ohio is impressed by the quality and increasing numbers of global children's books becoming available in her local library and bookstore. She also believes that her students, while living in a town with few international residents, will need to learn about countries beyond their national boundaries as they inevitably come into contact with our shrinking world. Also, they all come from families who once were immigrants to this country, and they will be enriched by the knowledge they gain about their own and others' heritage. Mindful also that an important topic in her social studies curriculum is study of Ohio, this teacher explores with her students connections between the state and other countries. Ohio happens to have many cities and towns named for ones in countries around the world, like Athens, Berlin, Calcutta, Damascus, Dublin, Hebron, Lima, Lisbon, Milan, Toledo, Vienna, and Warsaw. She sees this circumstance as a unique opportunity to study such cities and their home countries. Sharing children's books—novels and poetry, folktales, and informational books—with her students about these countries helps to increase their knowledge about those places and their understanding of the people and cultures. She truly enables these children to travel the world in their minds.

This teacher's vision was also Jella Lepman's dream. That great pioneer of international children's literature was passionate about the potential of books to further international understanding and world peace. Her ideas (1969), first proposed in the devastating aftermath of World War II, and relentless pursuit of her dream for an International Youth Library remain as relevant today as they were more than a half century ago. Current events remind us daily that human tendencies to divide ourselves into ever more sharply defined subgroups pervade our thinking. Although cultural identity is essential and important, our global future cannot afford the restrictions of narrow, exclusive ethnic, political, or religious enclaves. Now, as then, rigidity, smugness, or self-satisfaction with our own way of life and we–they dichotomies are dangerous for everyone. Children's books *can* bridge cultures, as Lepman argued, and as we have tried to demonstrate in the first four chapters.

In this final chapter, we focus on strategies to bring children and global books together so that intercultural bridges can be built. Specifically, we describe ways that classroom teachers can share international books in their work with children through (1) integrated studies centered on particular themes;

Jella Lepman

A true internationalist, Jella Lepman was originally a native of Stuttgart, Germany, where she worked as a journalist before World War II. However, because she was Jewish, she emigrated to Great Britain with her children in 1939. There, during the war, she worked for the BBC, the American Broadcasting Station in Europe, and the British Foreign Office. When World War II ended, the U.S. Army asked her to return to Germany as Special Advisor for Women's and Youth Affairs in the American zone, an assignment she finally accepted with reservations.

Thus, Lepman found herself at the Bad Homburg army headquarters, without a clear idea of what her job was to be. She immediately embarked on a fact-finding journey through Germany to determine what needs she could meet. Before long, she decided that her main goal would be to bring books to the children of Germany, where such books no longer existed. Through sheer persistence, determination, and the help of several well-placed friends (most notably Eleanor Roosevelt), Lepman accomplished her first major project in 1946—an International Exhibition of Children's Books with donations from many countries. The exhibit was housed in a former Nazi headquarters building in Munich and later toured through other major German cities.

Not willing to let the exhibit disband, Lepman conceived of an International Youth Library, for which she solicited and received help from the Pentagon, the Rockefeller Foundation, and the American Library Association. (Mildred Batchelder was another of Lepman's supporters.) Finally, the permanent International Youth Library opened in 1949 in Munich. Under Lepman's guidance, it soon developed many innovative programs for child patrons, including a story hour, child-authored book reviews, children's book discussion groups, foreign language instruction with children's books, a children's theater collaborative, book quizzes, parent teas, puppet shows, children's film screenings, an art studio for children, and a Children's United Nations.

Jella Lepman

This exciting literary and cultural center began to attract visitors and employees from around the world, and, in 1951, Lepman planned an international conference for professionals—writers, artists, librarians, teachers, publishers, and booksellers—interested in children's literature. At that conference, the International Board on Books for Young People was born, and Zürich, Switzerland, became its home. One of IBBY's signature accomplishments, the Hans Christian Andersen Award, came to be known as "the little Nobel Prize" and the most prestigious international recognition of children's literature. Lepman herself received this medal in 1956 in honor of her contribution to international children's books.

IBBY and the International Youth Library remain today as Lepman's permanent legacy and her vision of children's books as a bridge to international understanding. As she wrote, "Many of the best children's books had been translated into all languages and thus had become the common property of children throughout the world. The children had made them their own and had forgotten the lands they came from" (1969, p. 58). In her eyes, children's books were the best ambassadors for world peace for the next generation.

(2) examination of language to develop oral and written communication; (3) curricular connections that incorporate literature in content learning; (4) genre studies that enhance children's literary experience; and (5) illustrations that promote visual literacy.

Theme Studies

In a theme study children investigate a concept, idea, or topic in an integrated and interrelated manner. Active learning and inquiry are emphasized as children delve into different aspects of the theme across the curriculum. Global children's books are wonderful resources in theme studies. Books from many cultures in varied genres provide multiple perspectives on a theme and afford children the opportunity to explore the theme's content and concepts in depth. Two themes will be discussed in this section—"Everyday Life" for primary grades and "Journeys" for upper elementary grades. The discussion of these themes is not intended to be a comprehensive plan to implement a theme study, but rather to show how international books can effectively be incorporated in theme studies.

Everyday Life

This theme for children in grades K–3 develops the concept: The daily lives of children around the world share many similarities but also differ in significant ways. Global books enable teachers to help children move beyond superficial, obvious vestiges of culture such as food and clothing to a deeper understanding of relationships, values, and lifestyle.

As described in Chapter 4, the picture book by Tsubakiyama, *Mei-Mei Loves the Morning* (1999), set in contemporary China, captures a young girl's daily morning routine in which she and her grandpa bicycle with their bird Bai-Ling to a city park where "their friends are waiting at their favorite bench beneath the plum tree." The universal loving relationship between Mei-Mei and her grandfather is described within a specific cultural context and by recounting the things they do together in the morning.

Another picture book, Hidaka's *Girl from the Snow Country* (1986) is translated from the Japanese by Amanda Mayer Stincheum and follows the day in the life of a young Japanese girl, Mi-chan, who walks in the snow with her mother to market. As Mi-chan and her mother visit each stall, U.S. children learn the kinds of things sold in a Japanese village market: rice flour, rice-flour dogs, fish, crabs, and flowers. The girl returns home with red berries to use as eyes for the snow rabbits she has made. Hikada's soft watercolor illustrations give readers a glimpse into wintry Japanese village life. Mi-chan, like Mei-Mei, is portrayed in a loving relationship with a family member and is shown engaged in ordinary events of her life. Mei-Mei enjoys going to the park; Mi-chan relishes creating bunnies out of snow. American children could discuss the things they like to do, comparing activities with those in the stories.

The informational picture book *My Mama's Little Ranch on the Pampas* by Brusca (1994) transports children to Argentina where the author grew up. Brusca's text and watercolor illustrations create daily life on the ranch. Writing in the first person, the young girl (the author herself) describes the kinds of activities that occur throughout the seasons and helps American children realize that July is winter in the southern hemisphere. The end pages include a map of South America, a diagram depicting the difference in seasons, and other information.

Children can list the activities that occur on the ranch during the different seasons and illustrate some of these. They can also identify other parts of the world where July is winter.

A final picture book, *My Rows and Piles of Coins* (Mollel, 1999) depicts well everyday life in Tanzania. Based upon the author's childhood experiences, the story recounts Saruni's pride at helping his mother, Yeyo, carry goods to market, run errands, and do chores. As a reward, she gives him a few coins each week. Instead of spending them, Saruni saves the coins week after week to buy a new bicycle he found at the market. However, when Saruni's anticipated day arrives, he discovers that his 30 shillings and 50 cents is not nearly enough to pay for the new bike. Saruni's disappointment turns to joy the next day when Murete comes home

Tololwa M. Mollel

Tololwa Mollel, currently a U.S. resident, was born in Tanzania and lived with his grandparents on their coffee farm. The oral tradition of his Arusha Maasai roots flourished in that setting among his extended family and particularly his storytelling grandfather (Hile, 1997). Later, he lived in Canada and earned his master's degree from the University of Alberta, where he gained new appreciation for his literary heritage. Back in Tanzania, he taught theatre at the University of Dar es Salaam and told stories through his acting and directing of a local children's theatre group. Soon he began to write his own stories.

Mollel's first book, *Rhino's Boy* (1988) is a Maasai legend, and *Orphan Boy* (1991) is one of the old tales his grandfather told him as a boy. More retellings of myth and folklore followed, and Mollel reached beyond his own traditions to the Akamba people of East Africa in *The Princess Who Lost Her Hair: An Akamba Legend* (1993), the Igbo of Nigeria in *The Flying Tortoise: An Igbo Tale* (1994), and the Ashanti of Ghana in *Ananse's Feast: An Ashanti Tale* (1996).

Other stories, while blending elements from folklore, have contemporary settings, such as *Big Boy* (1995), about a young child's universal desire to be big enough to do the

things that his older brother can do instead of taking a nap, a wish that is granted by the magical bird, Tunukia-zawadi. Likewise, in *Subira Subira* (2000), Tatu seeks help from an old spirit woman in curing her young brother's hateful behavior.

Mollel's writing shows a third trend in realistic stories based upon his own childhood experiences, such as *Kele's Secret* (1997) about young Yoanes who follows his grandmother's most unusual hen to find where she lays her eggs and must conquer his fear of Grandfather's spooky shed to locate the nest. *My Rows and Piles of Coins* (1999), described in Chapter 5, is another story from Mollel's personal experience.

Mollel's books have been published in Australia, Great Britain, South Africa, and Canada, in addition to the United States. After teaching in Tanzania, he lived in Edmonton, Alberta, Canada for a number of years, where he was a writer-in-residence for the Edmonton Public Library and conducted workshops and gave storytelling presentations throughout Canada and the United States. This multinational author now lives in Minneapolis, Minnesota.

Jacket illustration copyright © 1999 by E. B. Lewis from *My Rows and Piles of Coins* by Tololwa M. Mollel.
Used with permission of Clarion Books.

with a new motorbike and offers to sell his old bicycle to Saruni. Then as a reward for Saruni's help, his parents give the money back to him. Mollel's storytelling voice is apparent in the repetition of Saruni's money counting: "I emptied the box, arranged all the coins in piles and the piles in rows. Then I counted the coins and thought about the bicycle I longed to buy." In addition, both Swahili and Maasai terms, such as *pikipiki* for motorbike, are sprinkled throughout the text and explained in an author's note. E. B. Lewis's full-page and double-spread watercolor paintings help readers envision the East African setting and 1960s time period.

These picture book representations of daily life can be complemented by informational photo-essays that take U.S. children to various parts of the world. Barbara Margolies traveled to the Maasai village of Olbalbal, Tanzania, to write and photograph *Olbalbal: A Day in Maasailand* (1994), with a brief introductory comment by Ambassador A. B. Nyakyi, permanent representative of Tanzania to the United Nations. In this photo-essay, Margolies follows the day of Kisululu, a 6-year-old boy who lives in the village with his mother, father, and siblings. "Kisululu's day begins when the sun fills the eastern sky. His mother collects wood for the fire" (p. 15). His day ends as he helps "bring his father's animals inside the *enkang*" (p. 32). Color photographs are explained in detailed captions that contain additional information. Children can write stories about a day in their own lives.

Kisululu's life can be compared to that of Armando and Gaspár, brothers who live in the town of Teabo on the Yucatan Peninsula in Mexico. Their daily life is documented in *Mayeros: A Yucatec Maya Family* (1997) by George Ancona, whose heritage is Mayan. Through color photographs and text, Ancona presents daily life in the village. Readers see the boys eating, reading, fetching firewood, and listening to grandfather tell a story. An author's note explains additional historical information about the Maya, and a glossary of Spanish and Yucatec words is provided. Children can write a compare/contrast essay either comparing the life of Kisululu and Armando or comparing the life of one of the boys to their own.

Another photo-essay focuses on one aspect of daily life, the games children enjoy playing and watching. *Baseball in the Barrios* by Horenstein (1997) introduces readers to 9-year-old Hubaldo who lives in Caracas, Venezuela, and loves baseball. American children whose summers are spent playing and watching this prevalent sport learn about its popularity in Venezuela, also. Instead of tee-ball and Little League, Hubaldo tells about Infantils, Preparatories, and Preinfantils. A glossary of baseball vocabulary in English and Spanish is included. This book lends itself well to a venn diagram about baseball in which children can show the similarities and differences in the sport as it is played in Venezuela and the United States.

Many learning experiences follow from reading these books that support this "Everyday Life" theme. Pen pals in other countries are now possible through e-mail as well as traditional letter writing. Children engage in map skills as they identify the countries in the books on maps and globes. Discussions about why children's lives in other countries may differ from their own guide American children to understand how climate, natural resources, economics, and heritage may influence a child's daily life.

Journeys

As mentioned in Chapter 2, a theme with an international focus for upper elementary grades is "Journeys," which children can explore both literally and metaphorically. The multilayered meanings of this theme can be quite abstract, with the main concept to be developed: Throughout life, we each embark on journeys, both physical and metaphorical, that may lead us to new destinations, new awakenings within ourselves, and new understandings about our world.

This theme could be introduced with the picture book *Caravan* by McKay (1995) about a 10-year-old Afghan boy who is able to travel for the first time in the caravan with his father on a 125-mile journey to the regional capital to trade felts and furs for grain. Darryl Ligasan's acrylic painted illustrations were inspired by photographs that appeared in a 1977 French book, *Caravans to Tartary* by Roland and Sabrina Michaud. *Caravan* well reflects both the literal and metaphoric nature of the theme. The story, written from the first-person perspective of Jura, the boy, indicates that "it is the day I become a man, and ride beside my father." Thus, Jura's journey over the mountains not only contributes to the economic well-being of his tribe but also symbolizes his coming of age. Children can begin the discussion of kinds of journeys people take in life and the importance of these journeys for signaling life passages. A chart of journeys that are studied—their destinations and purposes—can be started and developed throughout the theme. Children will no doubt be fascinated to learn about this kind of modern-day caravan and may brainstorm other types of caravans. An author's note explains that the Kirghiz, a nomadic people, live in the mountains of Afghanistan. Twice each winter, they travel across the mountains to trade, a journey that takes them 10 days. The author also defines words that may be unfamiliar to the reader such as *chogun* (a small teapot) and *yurt* (a circular tent).

British authors Martin and Tanis Jordan guide us to *Angel Falls: A South American Journey* (1995). Through Tanis's text and Martin's richly colored, realistic oil paintings, readers join this couple in Venezuala as they "travel up the Carroao River to a mountain called Auyantepui. Hidden in one of its canyons is the highest waterfall in the world, Angel Falls" (p. 7). Students can map the river, following the course of the journey and indicating the animals that the Jordans see along the way. They can also do further research on Angel Falls and the Carroao River to compile a "Fact Sheet" to accompany the book. This might include such facts as the height of the waterfall, who first "discovered it," and similar questions the children may seek to answer. The authors' "Glossary of Animals in this Book" could also serve as the beginning of further inquiry about the unusual animals that are mentioned. Children can also speculate why the couple, described on the book jacket as "ordinary people who just happen to like exploring," would take such a trip and can share places they would like to explore if provided the opportunity.

Another actual journey was taken by 9-year-old Sonam, whose story is documented in the photo-essay *Our Journey from Tibet: Based on a True Story* by Dolphin (1997). Since the occupation of Tibet by China over 40 years ago, His Holiness the Dalai Lama, the Tibetan spiritual and political leader, has lived in exile in India, where schools have been established to preserve Buddhism and Tibetan culture. With her sisters, Sonam leaves her family to make the illegal and difficult journey over the Himalayan mountains to India and the Tibetan Children's Village. Dolphin and photographer Nancy Jo Johnson present Sonam's journey, written in the first person from Sonam's perspective. A message from His Holiness the Fourteenth Dalai Lama and an afterward by Rinchen K. Choegyal, Minister-in-Charge of Education for the Tibetan government in exile, are included. Many American children have left their homelands, some for reasons similar to Sonam's. This book serves as a fine starting point for discussion about the exoduses of contemporary children.

Several fine novels with international settings reflect the journeys theme. Laird's *Kiss the Dust* (1991), winner of several British children's book awards, follows the escape of 13-year-old Tara and her father from Iraq, where her father participates in the Kurdish resistance. The family flees to Iran and eventually to London. Lehr (1995) shared this book with a group of fourth graders. Two boys become "totally absorbed" and made a "bas-relief map of Kurdistan" (p. 119). One of them wrote his final overall impressions of the book:

> Although this was my second 200 or more page book it felt like it was the best one I would ever read. One other thing is that it was weird how they had so little money but traveled so far. They started out in Iraq, went up into the Zangros Mountains which are mountains in Iran, then they went to a camp just north of the Zangros, then they escaped from that camp . . . then they flew to England. (p. 122)

Tara's journey to freedom for political reasons can be compared to the journey of Nhambo who flees from an undesired arranged marriage in Farmer's *A Girl Named Disaster* (1996). This award-winning book, set in Zimbabwe and Mozambique, is described in Chapter 4 and pairs well with *Kiss the Dust*. Children can create maps and track the journeys of the girls. The reasons for the journeys, the character traits of both girls, and the resolutions to their situations can all be compared. In addition, students can assume the perspective of one of the girls and write diary entries about her experiences. Both books may prompt the desire for research. For *Kiss the Dust*, children may investigate the Kurdish people, their history, and their persecution. For *A Girl Named Disaster*, children may inquire about tribal African religious beliefs and the still-contemporary practice of arranged marriages.

After children have read these books, they can return to the journeys chart that they started at the beginning of the theme. Children can compare and contrast these journeys—which are real or fictional, the varied purposes they served, and the obstacles that were overcome. They can then write an account of a journey that they have taken and create a visual representation of the journey. In addition, children can seek additional information about various journeys taken by contemporary children by contacting via letter or the Internet such organizations as Save the

Children Federation, UNICEF, or the International Rescue Committee. Finally, children can generate additional questions about journeys that they may wish to investigate such as journeys into space, journeys of exploration, and historical journeys to freedom.

The Beauty and Power of Language

Language is both beautiful and powerful. Hundreds of languages exist around the globe and each has its own distinctive sounds, patterns, rhythms, and lexicon. Language can entertain, soothe, convince, hurt, and inform. We express thoughts, feelings, and ideas through oral language and written communication. Jobe (1993) points out what he calls "language markers," language patterns that are distinctive to a given culture. These include names, such as *princess* or *sultan*, specific expressions, dialogue patterns, and storytelling patterns such as rhythm and onomatopoeia. He suggests that children examine these markers to gain insights into a culture. Global children's books afford children many opportunities for oral and written language development.

Cumulative tales can be a source for children's oral retelling and for writing of tales. According to Cullinan and Galda (1994), in a cumulative tale, "each incident grows from the preceding one . . . The initial incident reveals both central character and problem; each subsequent scene builds onto the original one. The accumulation continues to the climax and then unravels in reverse order or stops with an abrupt or surprise ending" (p. 179). The humor of these tales, which is often enhanced by their cumulativeness, has made them quite popular with children and gives teachers a venue to discuss how language works and how words and phrases can be patterned together. The Russian tale, *The Gigantic Turnip* by Tolstoy (1999), is the humorous tale of an old man and old woman who try to pick their turnip from the garden. They enlist the help of many animals, but the turnip "would not move." Finally, when the old woman catches a mouse to help them, "Pop! The gigantic turnip came flying out of the ground and everyone fell over." The repetitive language and the cumulative nature of the story lend themselves well to young children's oral retelling. In this version, originally published in the United Kingdom with illustrations by Niamh Sharkey, words and phrases are repeated and the pattern of the story is circular. In addition to oral retelling, this story serves as a good model for children to compose their own written cumulative tale.

An original cumulative tale first published in Switzerland, *Snail Started It!* by Reider (1997) tells how Snail insulted Pig and thereby started a chain of insults among the animals. When Goose tells Snail, "You are the slowest creature I've ever met!" Snail remembers insulting Pig and begins a new chain reaction of apologies. Colorful illustrations by Angela von Roehl represent the animals in this fanciful story, which lends itself well to dramatizing and choral reading.

Another folktale pattern, the pourquoi tale, provides the basis for both oral language experiences and writing. Aardema's (1995) pourquoi or "why" tale

How the Ostrich Got Its Long Neck "describes how an animal or person came to have a particular characteristic or how a certain natural phenomenon came to be." The Akamba tale explains how the short-necked ostrich tried to pull out crocodile's bad tooth with her beak. But when crocodile tries to eat ostrich, the battle to free herself results in ostrich's neck getting stretched longer and longer. In Aardema's retelling, many wonderful sounding words and phrases are used such as "tih tih tih," and "kwark! kwark!" making the story ideal for young children to chime in during oral reading or their own retelling. For a writing activity, Pratt and Beaty (1999) suggest that teachers "can choose an animal indigenous to their particular part of the United States and ask students to write individual or group stories explaining the origin of an animal's salient attributes, such as a squirrel's large bushy tale" (p. 33).

Books serve as models for different kinds of writing. Children can write directions to their favorite game using Lankford's *Dominoes Around the World* (1998) as a model. In this book, detailed directions for playing domino variants from Cuba, France, Malta, the Netherlands, Spain, Ukraine, Vietnam, and the United States are accompanied by a full-color illustrated scene painted by Karen Dugan. These scenes depict individuals from the culture playing dominoes. Children can individually or in pairs write directions to their favorite game and illustrate it. These directions can then be compiled into a class book of "Our Favorite Games."

Children writing alphabet books about various cultures, traditions, and countries combines their content knowledge with writing. *Gathering the Sun: An Alphabet in Spanish and English* by Ada (1997) provides a strong model for this kind of writing. The alphabet follows the Spanish "Árboes (trees). . . . Zanahoria (carrot)," thus also supporting children's familiarity with a language other than English. For Spanish-speaking children in the United States, this book works especially well to bridge home and school language use and meaning. All the words in the book relate to nature and working in the fields, and the Spanish is written in poetry. Each page of Ada's text is enhanced by gouache illustrations in rich tones of red, blue, and green by Simón Silva.

Another example of a bilingual text, Winter's *Diego* (1991) describes the childhood of the famous Mexican artist who lived from 1886 to 1957. Amy Prince translated the English into Spanish in this picture-book biography for primary-aged children. Jonah Winter's text is complemented by Jeanette Winter's illustrations in deep, rich colors. Each illustration resembles a miniature framed painting with its own border. This book would lend itself to a reader's theatre experience for young children in either English or Spanish as they orally tell about Diego's life.

Through global literature, children learn about the specific vocabulary of various languages and how vocabulary gives us insight into aspects of the culture. One of the poetry books discussed in Chapter 4, *Under the Breadfruit Tree* by Gunning (1998), contains a glossary of words found in the poems. In her introduction, Gunning explains, "In Jamaica the languages and culture are a rich mixture of African, East Indian, Chinese, and European influences. Both English and Creole are spoken, and this is reflected in the 'patois,' or everyday speech of the people" (p. 5). Children can begin to discuss how languages evolve and change and how American English has been influenced by all the languages brought to the United States by immigrants.

Many international folktales are available on audiotape read aloud by professional storytellers. Children enjoy listening to these tales told aloud when they can hear the beauty and cadence of language. For example, Laurence Yep's book, *The Rainbow People* (1989), a collection of 20 Chinese folktales, is available unabridged through Recorded Books. August House specializes in bringing folklore and storytelling to children. The audiotape, "Multicultural Tales to Tell" (1994), contains 20 folktales from around the world. Countries represented include Germany, China, Tibet, Korea, and Africa, offering many folktales.

Through experiences with global literature that emphasize oral and written language, children gain appreciation for the richness of languages around the world and further develop their own language abilities.

Content Connections

The number of teachers incorporating children's literature in content areas across the elementary curriculum has gained momentum in recent years. Teachers find that children's curiosity and interest are heightened by sharing well-crafted and visually appealing books. Children's books in the content areas provide multiple perspectives on a topic, in-depth coverage, and a way to meet individual differences in reading ability. Global children's books can also support content and concepts across the curriculum. In this section a few examples of books for math, science, and social studies will be shared.

Math

One Grain of Rice: A Mathematical Folktale by Demi (1997) is a folktale from India that helps children to vividly understand the power of doubling. In this tale, a raja had collected rice from the people each year and then distributed back to them only "enough rice to get by." When famine comes, the people are unable to give rice to the raja and therefore have little rice to eat. Although the people implore, the raja refuses to open the royal storehouse to give people rice. Then Rani, a clever village girl, devises a plan to ensure rice for the people. As a reward for returning some fallen rice to the raja, Rani requests, "Today, you will give me a single grain of rice. Then, each day for thirty days you will give me double the rice you gave me the day before. Thus, tomorrow you will give me two grains of rice, the next day four grains of rice, and so on for thirty days." Upper elementary students are challenged to calculate how many grains of rice Rani will receive in a month. A chart at the end of the book can be consulted for students to verify their calculations.

Younger children will be intrigued by *Emeka's Gift: An African Counting Story* by Onyefulu (1995). Originally published in Great Britain, this informational book uses a counting format to present information about the Igala tribe of Nigeria.

Color photographs illustrate each of the numbers, which are written as a numeral and in words to reinforce counting from 1 to 10. The number one stands for "One boy . . . His name was Emeka." The book then continues "Two of Emeka's friends," . . . "Ten of Emeka's cousins." Sidebars provide additional information about the culture such as markets, necklaces, and ishaka (musical instruments). Children can fashion their own counting books either with new illustrations for this story or with a counting book about themselves.

Science

The study of animals occurs throughout the elementary years. Robert Bateman's *Safari* (1998), originally published in Canada, gives children a wonderful introduction to African animals in an accessible format. Bateman, a former geography and art teacher, is a painter who has traveled to Africa several times. He invites readers to travel on this safari and to "leave your modern life behind and listen to the rhythm of the land." Each double-page spread features an animal with magnificent lifelike paintings about the animal, accompanied by informative text and a box of specific data about the animal, including habitat, height, weight, food, and range. This enables children to compare and contrast the animals on specific factors. Some of the animals, such as the elephant, leopard, and giraffe, are familiar to children, while others may be newly introduced, for example, the wildebeest, lesser kudu, and impala. At the book's conclusion, the author tells readers the importance of "saving wild places."

Another book about animals, Lasky's *Shadows in the Dawn: The Lemurs of Madagascar* (1998), transports readers to the island of Madagascar to visit primatologist Alison Jolly, who studies lemurs. Author Kathryn Lasky and her husband, photographer Christopher Knight, took an expedition with Jolly where they experienced firsthand the events documented in this book. Children will learn about lemurs who live among the tamarind trees on the Berenty reserve in Madagascar, where they are protected. Lasky explains, "Like humans, lemurs are primates, mammals that share certain common traits, such as hands that are good at grasping, brains that are large in comparison to body size . . . " (p. 10). This book could be used in a more specialized study of mammals and primates. As in the Bateman book, Lasky writes an afterword appealing to readers to help with wildlife preservation and informing them about the Wildlife Preservation Trust International.

Lasky and Knight have also collaborated to present *Surtsey: The Newest Place on Earth* (1992), a book that relates to the science topics of volcanos and ecology. A volcanic eruption in the ocean off the coast of Iceland created the island of Surtsey in 1963. Lasky and Knight received special permission to visit Surtsey in order to research this book. In carefully documented, clear text and magnificent photographs, most of which were taken by Knight, readers learn about the formation of an island, facts about lava, and how a new island is colonized by plant and animal life. This book is packed with fascinating information and reinforces how science continues to add new understandings about our world.

Social Studies

Many upper elementary classrooms include exploration of peace studies and ways to promote peace. A unique book compiled by Sheila Hamanaka, *On the Wings of Peace* (1995), includes writings and artwork about peace by 60 authors and illustrators around the world. The book is subtitled, "Writers and Illustrators Speak Out for Peace in Memory of Hiroshima and Nagasaki," and Hamanaka wrote an introduction to explain the background and purpose of the book. Royalties are donated to several peace organizations: Amnesty International USA, For our Children's Sake Foundation, and Friends of Hibakusha. Authors are from Chile, South Africa, Haiti, Japan, Denmark, United Kingdom, Iran, Canada, Brazil, Poland, and Guatemala as well as the United States.

Citizenship is an important concept within the elementary curriculum. Oftentimes, American children take the democratic process and open access to voting for granted. In the picture book, *The Day Gogo Went to Vote* by Sisulu (1996), described in Chapter 4, a young South African girl narrates the story about her Gogo (great-grandmother) voting for the first time in her life. In 1994, Black South Africans were finally given the right to vote in a national election. Older children can compare this story to the struggle of women and blacks in the United States to gain the right to vote.

Another social studies topic for fifth or sixth grade is the Middle Ages. Originally published in England, Sheila Sancha's *Walter Dragun's Town: Crafts and Trades in the Middle Ages* (1989), a carefully researched informational book, takes readers to Stanford, England, in 1274. Here children meet the men and women of this medieval town who are engaged in all types of occupations as well as those in power such as "Walter Dragun, the most unpopular man in Stanford" (p. 16). Sancha's detailed line drawings visually represent the daily life described in the text. The end matter includes "The Names," which explains the origins of names mentioned in the text and a glossary. Children can compare the kinds of occupations prevalent in the Middle Ages to those of contemporary society. This book can also serve as a springboard for a process drama in which students assume the roles of various townspeople.

These suggestions are examples of some ways that global children's literature can support specific content in the elementary curriculum. Books are a valuable resource to introduce content and concepts, enhance the development of ideas, and extend children's thinking. They open opportunities for children to demonstrate their knowledge of what they have learned and to represent that knowledge in many forms.

Genre Study

A solid grasp of the genres described in Chapter 4 provides a foundation for literary study, an educated form of reader response that can enhance both individual and collective literary experiences. In this section, we use juxtapositions of pairs or groups of books—even texts that may initially appear quite unlike each other, such as different genres—to highlight reader awareness of literary elements that may go unnoticed by considering each work alone (Lehman & Crook, 1998).

Plot, Character

Two novels for middle-grade children offer excellent comparisons of plot and character. Kazumi Yumoto's *The Friends* (1996), to which we have referred earlier, was winner of the Mildred Batchelder award and selected for the IBBY 1998 Honour List for translation. This realistic account depicts the escapades of three sixth-grade Japanese boys—Kiyama, Kawabe, and Yamashita. Their natural curiosity about what happens when a person dies and their need for diversion from the stress of summer cram school prompt the trio to spy on an elderly neighbor whose death they believe is imminent. This man puts the boys to work repairing his dilapidated house and weeding his overgrown garden. Gradually, the boys' interest changes to a deep sense of caring for the old man, and when he eventually dies, the boys realize that they have learned more from him about living than about dying.

Skellig, by David Almond (1999) and recipient of the 1999 Carnegie Medal in Great Britain, has supernatural elements within a realistic setting. The narrator, Michael, and his parents have just moved into a "handyman special" house, and his baby sister, born prematurely, is struggling to survive. In the crumbling garage, Michael discovers a strange winged being, who introduces himself as Skellig, apparently near death, covered by cobwebs, dust, and dead flies. Michael also makes a new friend, his neighbor, Mina, in whom he confides about Skellig, and together they move him to a safer hiding place. Their care for this beast-bird-angel restores Skellig's life, and he, in turn, transmits life to the baby sister.

These two novels, both portraying children's resourcefulness in caring for someone initially dependent and unlovable, pose intriguing comparisons. They show youngsters assuming responsibilities usually carried by adults, and in *Skellig*, Michael and Mina even try to hide the creature from adults they believe will harm him. Both books show children dealing with issues of life and death: *The Friends* first study and then mourn the old man's death, and Michael and his parents fear for his baby sister's life. Michael even asks Skellig to wish for the baby's survival. However, within these serious plots, there are humorous events, such as the friends' pranks on the old man and his table-turning on them and the banter between Michael and Mina or his friends, Coot and Leakey.

The characters in these books share some common traits, such as similarity in age and the same childlike morbid fascination with things that would repulse most adults. This interest also is what compels them to provide the care that adults obviously have ignored. In addition, they demonstrate many of the same developmental interests in play, imagination, and resourcefulness and the need to maintain part of their lives separate from adults. However, *The Friends* initially are downright mean to the old man, while Michael and Mina show compassion for Skellig from the start. Michael and Mina also are willing to believe in the supernatural qualities of this creature.

Middle-grade readers could contrast the narratives' events and resolutions, the mysterious backgrounds of the old man and Skellig, and the characters' traits. Readers could even examine what effect the addition of supernatural qualities has on the tone and mood of *Skellig* in comparison to *The Friends'* realism. Finally, children can compare these stories to their own friends and experiences.

Setting

Two novels for older readers allow intriguing considerations of the importance of time and place in story. Although both are historical fiction, these works take place nearly two centuries apart. Dorothy and Thomas Hoobler's *The Ghost in the Tokaido Inn* (1999) is set in eighteenth-century Japan, while *The Only Outcast* by Julie Johnston (1998) and originally published in Canada happens in early twentieth-century Canada. In *Ghost*, Seikei, age 14, yearns to become a samurai rather than settle for the unexciting life for which he is destined as a tea merchant's son. On a trade journey to the city of Edo with his father, Seikei stumbles upon adventure at the inn where they stop for the night. The theft of a priceless ruby and Seikei's glimpse of a ghost at the inn leads to Judge Ooka, who hears the case, enlisting Seikei to help solve the crime. Along the way, Seikei demonstrates the character of a true samurai and ultimately creates his own destiny.

Fred Dickson, age 16, leads a very different life, but there is suspense to his story, as well. The eldest of four children, Fred is small, awkward, uncertain, and worst of all for a teenager, a stutterer who feels like *The Only Outcast* in a world of accepted insiders, a feeling that is exacerbated by his father's lack of understanding. The children summer at their grandparents' cottage on Rideau Lake near Perth, Ontario—carefree days filled with the typical adventures of teenage boys, such as boating, fishing, swimming, and sleeping in a tent. However, this innocent existence takes on new dimensions when Fred falls for a beautiful girl vacationing at a nearby resort hotel and Fred's grandfather relates ghost stories about a murderous ferryman who had operated in the area about 80 years earlier. The connection between these two incidents creates an intriguing mystery that offers Fred the opportunity to prove himself and gain a sense of self-worth.

Readers can analyze what contributes to the development of setting in these two books. In *Ghost*, the time period of Japan ruled by the warrior samurai class and its code of honor, the traditions of kabuki theater, rigid customs governing life choices, and the Japanese view of outsiders (particularly Kirishitans, or Christians) all work together to create a definite sense of time and place. Likewise, for *Outcast*, Canadians' view of Americans who vacation at Rideau Lake clearly distinguishes this story's setting from a similar U.S. environment. In addition, the history of Canadian wilderness settlement provides the necessary backdrop for the ferryman mystery that plays a central role in this story. Overlaying it all, the watery expanses of the lake setting symbolically enhance the plot and themes. Once they begin this exploration, readers will discover these and many other factors that develop setting, and they can consider how radically different the stories would be if the settings were altered.

Style

Two books on the same topic—war—demonstrate the power of contrasting literary styles. British writer Neil Philip edited a collection of poetry, *War and the Pity of War* (1998), reflecting worldwide conflicts from ancient China and Greece to contemporary situations. There are ballads, epitaphs, traditional and free verses, and

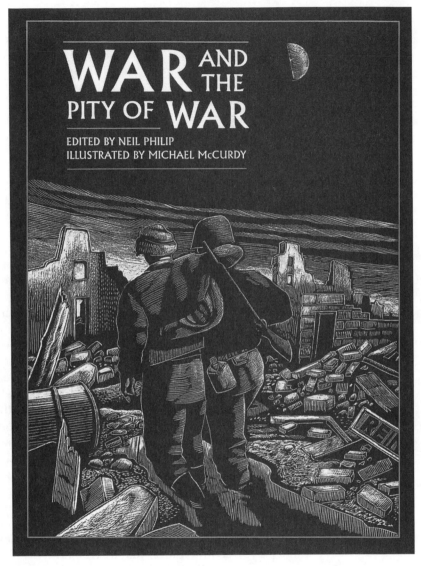

Jacket illustration copyright © 1998 by Michael McCurdy from *War and Pity of War* edited by Neil Philip. Used with permission of Clarion Books.

concrete poems. Most are sad or poignant, such as Dan Pagis's unfinished "Written in Pencil in the Sealed Railway-Car," about a transport of Jews during the Holocaust, but several show humor, such as W. H. Auden's "Roman Wall Blues." The range of poems, from Saga Nobuyuki's "The Myth of Hiroshima" to Ken Smith's bilingual "The Essential Serbo-Croat," demonstrates the universal tragedy of war. Michael McCurdy's stark black and white scratchboard illustrations fittingly accompany the book's overall somber tone.

Documentary filmmaker Maria Ousseimi, who grew up in Lebanon, drew upon her travels to wars in Lebanon, El Salvador, Mozambique, and Bosnia-Herzegovina to create *Caught in the Crossfire: Growing Up in a War Zone* (1995). In this informational account, she presents the perspectives of young people she interviewed on the wars that overshadowed their daily lives. Straightforward text, direct quotes in the children's voices, and haunting black and white photographs add a moving immediacy to the content. The last chapter about the battlefield of inner-city Washington, D.C., draws stark parallels between distant wars and current reality for some children in the United States.

These two works present opportunities to explore how different genres' style capture the same topic in contrasting, but deeply moving, ways. Older readers could discuss the effectiveness and purposes of poetry and expository text for conveying information or evoking emotion. They can consider how the different styles of the arresting illustrations in these books contribute to overall mood. Finally, readers can compare the nature of their own responses to differing styles.

Theme

Two picture books for younger readers present opportunities for comparing similar themes. In Karen Lynn Williams's *Painted Dreams* (1998), Ti Marie, a young Haitian longs for real paints and brushes to create the pictures she draws with any materials she can find, but her family is too poor to afford such luxuries. She scavenges leftover paint from the garbage of Msie Antoine, the village bocor (voodoo priest) and artist. With these paints, Ti Marie creates a lovely mural that attracts many customers to buy fruits and vegetables at her mother's formerly unnoticed market stall. Catherine Stock's watercolor illustrations complement Ti Marie's naive creations.

Delmore and his mother, Loretta, also have dreams in *Apple Batter* by Deborah Turney Zagwÿn (1999) from Canada. Delmore, a baseball fan, strives to become a good hitter, while Loretta, a gardener, plants three apple trees and yearns for a delicious harvest. Every day, Delmore practices and Loretta waits patiently, but bad weather and Delmore's improved aim doom Loretta's precious apples. Her love for her son helps Loretta overcome disappointment, and she makes apple crumble to celebrate his accomplishment.

Children can compare the similarity of the theme in these books: the importance of having and pursuing dreams in life. However, readers also can distinguish subtle nuances in the way that theme is portrayed. In *Painted Dreams*, Ti Marie's determination and ingenuity keep her from giving up in spite of her parents' inability to help her. In *Apple Batter*, Delmore's perseverance with daily batting practice enables him to attain the desired skill. While both characters are responsible for their own achievements, in each case, the child also receives support and encouragement from an adult: Ti Marie's father and Msie Antoine recognize her talent, and Loretta understands Delmore's wish and shows pride in his success even as her own dream fails. Finally, readers can relate this theme to their own experiences.

Point of View

A picture book from a South African team offers opportunities for readers to experiment with point of view. Dianne Stewart employs an omniscient narrator to reveal the different perspectives of two characters in *Gift of the Sun: A Tale from South Africa* (1996), originally published in Great Britain. Lazy Thulani makes a series of decisions to eliminate his work and attempt to please his wife, Dora: selling the cow and buying a goat, selling the goat and buying a sheep, and so on. However, each action brings criticism from Dora, who believes that Thulani makes poor choices. Their differing viewpoints on the chain of events create humor and eventually unite in a satisfying conclusion. Jude Daly's paintings create a contemporary rural setting for this story.

Likewise, in *Apple Batter*, described above, Delmore and Loretta's points of view present two impressions about the fate of the apples. The illustrations further develop this comparison by visually depicting on the same page the two characters engaged in separate activities that preoccupy their attention. In fact, one double-page spread even contains labels that explicitly identify "Loretta's focus" and "Delmore's focus." Children can contrast how the two different characters in these books see the narrative's events. They could retell or rewrite the story entirely from one character's point of view, thereby discovering how that would change the narrative. They could dramatize the double perspectives by creating a reader's theater version of the story in two, first-person voices. Older children might even grasp how perspective can contribute irony and humor in literature.

These examples of genre study are intended to demonstrate how exploring literary elements with children in developmentally appropriate ways can enrich their response to and experience with literature. Teachers can facilitate such exploration by listening closely to children's responses and building upon those ideas to nudge children's thinking to a more critical level. In discussions, teachers can ask genuine, open-ended, higher-order questions that relate children's insights (probably indirectly) to literary concepts. Beyond the limitations of the brief presentations about books provided in this chapter, extensive reading and study of the literature of particular cultures may provide insights about how plots and characters are developed, the relative importance of setting, unique styles, what kinds of themes are especially meaningful, and how point of view is used in specific regions of the world. (For further specific teaching ideas, teachers might consult Ron Jobe's [1993] helpful resource, *Cultural Connections: Using Literature to Explore World Cultures with Children.*) Adults knowledgeable about literature and how to build on children's responses can cultivate young people's growth as readers and their understanding of world literatures.

Visual Literacy

Reading pictures and photographs is vital to comprehending and appreciating many genres of children's literature. Stewig (1992) notes critics' and teachers' lack of attention to illustrations and argues for the importance of visual literacy to the total literary experience. Children themselves may be more discerning viewers than are many adults; they can read pictures before words and most likely have grown up in a highly visual environment. In this section, we consider how pictures in global literature help to tell stories or convey information, how they add details not provided in the text, how visual elements complement the work as a whole, and how artistic style complements the culture portrayed in the book.

Storytelling, Conveying Information

Perhaps, in a picture book, illustrations most obviously help to tell the story. Pierre Yves Njeng's paintings for *Vacation in the Village: A Story from West Africa* (1999) support the narrative about Nwemb, a young city boy, whose family decides to spend their vacation in his grandparents' village. Nwemb has never been there, and he hates leaving all his friends behind and worries about finding playmates in the village. The vacation turns out to be a wonderful adventure, although very different from city life. The pictures not only depict the story events and children's vacation activities, but also provide much information about the setting needed by readers unfamiliar with Cameroon. For example, the contrast between Nwemb's cosmopolitan life in the city and the more rustic, traditional village environment helps readers to understand Nwemb's feelings and also to realize the variety of contemporary lifestyles in this African country.

Michèle Solá's text and Jeffrey Jay Foxx's color photographs combine to convey information in *Angela Weaves a Dream: The Story of a Young Maya Artist* (1997), about a young Maya girl living in southern Mexico. For the first time, Angela will be entering the annual weaving contest in her village of San Andrés. Information about weaving and its place in her culture is interwoven with her ancestors' stories and prayers. The seven sacred designs are each shown in an enlarged photograph, with a sidebar drawing and explanation of the design's meaning. Other photos, accompanied by detailed captions, show weaving activities and village daily life. A photographic detail of Angela's design borders many pages, and the inclusion of maps showing Maya territory in the end matter provides more visual information. All the visual elements in this book highlight the importance of color and design in Maya culture, and appreciation of them is essential to the experience of this book.

Adding Details

In addition to reinforcing the narrative or exposition, illustrations often add details not given in the text. For example, in *Vacation,* described above, signs printed on the school building and train station are in French, signaling to viewers that Nwemb's culture speaks that language. In the picture of children play-hunting in the fields, we can identify the crop as corn. These touches add to our understanding of Cameroon.

From Canada comes Maxine Trottier's picture book about a Vietnamese man, Van, who carries *The Walking Stick* (1998) from the Buddhist temple where he found it until he flees the Vietnam war with his wife and daughter across the ocean to a new country. After his daughter marries a blond, blue-eyed man, their daughter absorbs all her grandfather's stories of his homeland. Eventually, she returns to the temple in Vietnam where she leaves the walking stick at the foot of the Buddha with a prayer of thanks for watching over her family's journey. Annouchka Gravel Galouchko's jewel-toned paintings contribute numerous symbolic details to this thoughtful tale, beginning with the richly patterned endpapers. In every illustration, intricate designs contain hidden faces and other symbols, such as eyes, fish, or dragons that evoke a sense of the setting, religion, and belief system of Vietnam. Young readers will enjoy the challenge of discovering these details and learning more about how they relate to the culture depicted.

Complementing the Work

Picture-book readers also can explore how artists deliberately use visual elements to complement the work as a whole. For example, in *The Gift* by Gabriela Keselman (1999), first published in Spain, layout for Pep Montserrat's bold illustrations contributes to the story's playful mood. This book, recipient of Spain's Generalitat de Catalunya Best Illustrated Book for Children and on the 1998 IBBY Honour List, portrays Mikie's wish for a special present from his parents—something very big, strong, soft, long-lasting, sweet, and warm, and able to rock from side to side and make him fly and laugh. At last, his puzzled parents, unable to think what gift he means, give Mikie a hug that meets all the criteria. The pages are arranged so that each picture of Mikie delivering one of his qualifications is positioned on the left side of the spread, while a folded page on the right shows his parents' reaction on the outside fold but conceals their idea of something that meets the characteristic depicted when the page is unfolded. This format allows readers to enjoy the game of predicting the parents' solutions and guessing the overall answer to Mikie's riddle. Children could create their own books using this design for original stories.

Willemien Min from the Netherlands effectively uses color to complement the mood of *Peter's Patchwork Dream* (1999), originally published in Holland, about a young boy who becomes bored while spending a sick day in bed. To occupy his thoughts, Peter imagines going for a walk across the fields of his patchwork quilt where he picks berries and apples, plays with bunnies, goes sailing, and waters flowers. Returning from his adventure, Peter finds his friends who have come to cheer him with a visit. Muted, earth-toned colors—blues, greens, golds, and browns with splashes of red—of the patchwork endpapers and story illustrations evoke the summary, country setting of this innocent adventure. They contrast markedly with the bright colors and bold black outlines of the cartoon-like illustrations in *The Gift*.

A picture book for middle-grade readers, *I'm José and I'm Okay (Three Stories from Bolivia)* by German author Werner Holzwarth (1999), uses illustrations and layout in a unique way to advance the stories in this collection. Three artists—Erlini Tola, Freddy Oporto, and Carlos Llanque—created the pictures for the organization, Yatiyawi Studios, that collaborated on the book's production. The stories—"José the Prankster," "José the Winner," and "José the Avenger"—follow the experiences of an 11-year-old orphan who makes some realistic choices and deals with the results. The paintings are grittily expressionistic, almost like street graffiti with heavy black lines and bold, fairly dark colors. Most double-page spreads use several pictures of different sizes and placement, overlaid with captions containing José's thoughts, which are integral to the stories. Viewers need to examine these dynamic illustrations carefully to understand how color, style, and layout all contribute meaning to the overall work and even what these elements might tell us about the culture of the story.

In *Jon's Moon* (1999) originally published in Spain, acclaimed author-illustrator Carme Solé Vendrell from Spain masterfully uses color and layout of the pictures to symbolically enhance the narrative. Jon and his father, a fisherman, live in a whitewashed cottage perched on a cliff by the sea. One night a terrible storm nearly kills his father as he is fishing, and when he returns home, he lies ill in bed under Jon's anxious watch. With the moon's help Jon courageously recovers his father's lost spirit from the ocean depths, thus restoring him to good health. The watercolor, airbrush, and pencil illustrations have white border frames on most pages. These paintings are placed opposite a page of text, for some of which a border is cleverly suggested by a fragment of illustration in the corner, for example, that fades to white for the rest of the page. However, in pictures of the ocean, the viewer's perspective is from sea level, looking back toward land, and the waves overflow the white borders, while the rest of the picture remains within the border. This graphically demonstrates the ocean's power. In addition, the underwater pictures have no borders, but bleed to the page edges, and one underwater double-page spread contains no text. Color also changes from a warm pink glow at the beginning to dark green, grey, black, and purple during the storm and spirit rescue and back to cheery bright yellow for the happy resolution. Children could compare how such elements as color and page frames are used in other books and how they convey meaning.

Complementing the Culture of the Work

Finally, artistic style often complements the culture portrayed in a picture book. For example, American author J. Alison James retells the story of *The Drums of Noto Hanto* (1999) about how the people of this Japanese village cleverly and courageously outwit a threatening warlord with their use of terrifying masks, bonfires, and pounding drums, creating a spectacle so frightening that the samurai retreat. Japanese-born Tsukushi, now an American resident, created the dramatic collage illustrations with cut paper in bright colors and varying textures to reflect the culture depicted in the narrative. The artwork also matches the theatrical style of the author's first encounter with this story as performed by a taiko drumming group. Readers can compare the art in this book with similar ones inspired by Asian settings, for example, Ed Young's work in *Hush: A Thai Lullaby* by Ho (1996a), or Grayce Bochak's illustrations for *The Long Silk Strand: A Grandmother's Legacy to Her Granddaughter* by Williams (1995).

In contrast, Mary Grandpré's lush illustrations for *The House of Wisdom*, by Florence Parry Heide and Judith Heide Gilliland (1999), reflect the culture of ninth-century Baghdad. This true story recounts a boy's quest to discover the key to the special joy his father, the Caliph's best translator in the great library, feels as he works with books that are brought from all over the world to this center of learning. Only after Ishaq leads an expedition to search for more books does he gain true understanding of the treasures of books. An authors' note explains that Ishaq went on to spend his life translating Aristotle's entire work. The art, as richly colored as tapestries, is designed to resemble ancient Islamic books with framed text boxes and page borders. Designs within the pictures also depict the architecture, tiles, and carpets of the Middle East. Middle-grade readers can be invited to compare other artwork inspired by this region for similarities.

Much of the potential for global literature to cross cultures lies in book illustrations. We have merely sampled some ways that pictures contribute to the meaning of these books. Through authentic activities and deft questioning, teachers can draw children's attention to such ideas as how illustrations help to tell stories or present information, how they give additional details not included in the text, how their artistic elements complement the work as a whole, and how their style reinforces the culture portrayed. By educating children's visual literacy, we can help young readers to greater appreciation and understanding not only of the individual works, but also for the cultures they represent.

Conclusion

When it comes to global children's literature, Susan Stan's (1999) words humble us. "The 'international' books presented to American children are only a small taste of children's literature worldwide . . . " (p. 175). The sampling of recent international books we have explored in this text is from titles written or translated in English and available in the United States. However, this tiny fraction of world children's literature is a beginning, and the more we know about these kinds of books and share them with children, the more we will demand, and other global books will surely follow. Through books, we can offer children the opportunity to travel to faraway places—like Great Aunt Arizona, in their minds, if not physically—and to realize Jella Lepman's dream to build bridges of international understanding for world peace.

REFERENCES

Abu-Nasr, J. (1996). The Arab world. In P. Hunt & S. Ray (Eds.), *International companion encyclopedia of children's literature* (pp. 789–794). New York: Routledge.

Anagnostopoulos, V. D. (1996). Greece. In P. Hunt & S. Ray (Eds.), *International companion encyclopedia of children's literature* (pp. 761–764). New York: Routledge.

Baillie, A. (1995). Pol Pot's reign of terror: Why write about it for children? In S. Lehr (Ed.), *Battling dragons: Issues and controversy in children's literature* (pp. 148–154). Portsmouth, NH: Heinemann.

Banks, J. A. (1999). *An introduction to multicultural education* (2nd ed.). Boston: Allyn and Bacon.

Batchelder, M. (1966). Learning about children's books in translation. *ALA Bulletin, 60,* 33–42.

Bishop, R. S. (1992). Multicultural literature for children: Making informed choices. In V. Harris (Ed.), *Teaching multicultural literature in grades K–8* (pp. 37–53). Norwood, MA: Christopher-Gordon.

Bogart, D. (Ed.). (1999). *The Bowker annual: Book trade almanac.* New Providence, NJ: R. R. Bowker.

Bosma, B. (1992). *Fairy tales, fables, legends and myths: Using folk literature in your classroom* (2nd ed.). New York: Teachers College Press.

Broderick, K. (1994). Talking translation: An interview with Dagmar Herrmann. *Book Links, 3*(3), 40.

Bunbury, R. M. (1996). Australia. In P. Hunt & S. Ray (Eds.), *International companion encyclopedia of children's literature* (pp. 843–854). New York: Routledge.

Carus, M. (1980). Translation and internationalism in children's literature. *Children's Literature in Education, 11,* 171–179.

Cianciolo, P. J. (1997). *Picture books for children* (4th ed.). Chicago: American Library Association.

Cotton, P. (1999). Picture books: A European perspective. *Journal of Children's Literature, 25*(1), 18–27.

Cullinan, B. E., & Galda, L. (1994). *Literature and the child* (3rd ed.). Fort Worth, TX: Harcourt Brace College.

Cullinan, B. E., & Galda, L. (1998). *Literature and the child* (4th ed.). Fort Worth, TX: Harcourt Brace College.

Daikiw, J. Y. (1990). Children's literature and global education: Understanding the developing world. *Reading Teacher, 43,* 296–300.

Diaz, C. F., Massialas, B. G., & Xanthopoulos, J. A. (1999). *Global perspectives for educators.* Boston: Allyn and Bacon.

Dyson, A. H., & Genishi, C. (1994). *The need for story: Cultural diversity in classroom and community.* Urbana, IL: National Council of Teachers of English.

Evans, C. S. (1987). Teaching a global perspective in elementary classrooms. *Elementary School Journal, 87,* 545–555.

Freeman, E. B. (1999). Uri Orlev: International storyteller. *Journal of Children's Literature, 25*(1), 44–47.

Gilderdale, G. (1996). New Zealand. In P. Hunt & S. Ray (Eds.), *International companion encyclopedia of children's literature* (pp. 855–861). New York: Routledge.

Gilliland, J. H. (1995). Living in Sami's and Ahmed's worlds: Picture books explore children's lives in other countries. In S. Lehr (Ed.), *Battling dragons: Issues and controversy in children's literature* (pp. 105–112). Portsmouth, NH: Heinemann.

Gray, P. (1999, September 20). Wild about Harry. *Time, 154,* 66–72.

Hancock, M. R. (2000). *A celebration of literature and response: Children, books, and teachers in K–8 classrooms.* Columbus, OH: Merrill.

Hanvey, R. G. (1976). *An attainable global perspective.* New York: Global Perspectives in Education.

Hazard, P. (1944). *Books, children & men.* Trans. M. Mitchell. Boston: Horn Book.

Heale, J. (1996). Africa: English-speaking Africa. In P. Hunt & S. Ray (Eds.), *International companion encyclopedia of children's literature* (pp. 795–801). New York: Routledge.

Hile, K. S. (Ed.). (1997). *Something about the author.* Vol. 88. Detroit: Gale.

Hirano, C. (1999). Eight ways to say you: The challenges of translation. *The Horn Book Magazine, 75,* 34–41.

Hopkins, L. B. (1987). *Pass the poetry, please!* (rev. ed.). New York: Harper.

Huck, C. (1989). No wider than the heart is wide. In J. Hickman & B. E. Cullinan (Eds.), *Children's literature in the classroom: Weaving Charlotte's Web* (pp. 252–262). Needham Heights, MA: Christopher-Gordon

Huck, C. S., Hepler, S., Hickman, J., & Kiefer, B. Z. (1997). *Children's literature in the elementary school* (6th ed.). Madison, WI: Brown & Benchmark.

International Relations Committee of the Association for Library Service to Children. (1998). Outstanding translated children's books: Birth of a bibliography by committee. *Journal of Youth Services in Libraries, 11,* 263–271.

Jaffa, M. (1996). The Indian sub-continent. In P. Hunt & S. Ray (Eds.), *International companion encyclopedia of children's literature* (pp. 807–822). New York: Routledge.

Jinguh, T. (1996). Japan. In P. Hunt & S. Ray (Eds.), *International companion encyclopedia of children's literature* (pp. 837–842). New York: Routledge.

Jobe, R. (1988). Profile: Patricia Crampton. *Language Arts, 65,* 410–414.

Jobe, R. (1990). Profile: Anthea Bell. *Language Arts, 67,* 432–438.

Jobe, R. (1993). *Cultural connections: Using literature to explore world cultures with children.* Markham, Ontario, Canada: Pembroke.

Jobe, R. (1996). Translation. In P. Hunt & S. Ray (Eds.), *International companion encyclopedia of children's literature* (pp. 519–529). New York: Routledge.

Khorana, M. (1996). Uri Orlev: Celebrating the indomitable spirit of childhood. *Bookbird, 34*(2), 6–8.

Kiefer, B. Z. (1995). *The potential of picturebooks: From visual literacy to aesthetic understanding.* Columbus, OH: Merrill.

Klingberg, G. (1986). *Children's fiction in the hands of translators.* Malmö, Sweden: CWK Gleerup.

Kniep, W. M. (1986). Defining a global education by its content. *Social Education, 50,* 437–446.

Lehman, B. A., & Crook, P. R. (1998). Doubletalk: A literary pairing of *The Giver* and *We are all in the dumps with Jack and Guy. Children's Literature in Education, 29,* 69–78.

Lehr, S. (1995). Fourth graders read, write, and talk about freedom. In S. Lehr (Ed.), *Battling dragons: Issues and controversy in children's literature* (pp. 114–140). Portsmouth, NH: Heinemann.

Lepman, J. (1969). *A bridge of children's books.* Chicago: American Library Association.

Lukens, R. J. (1999). *A critical handbook of children's literature* (6th ed.). New York: Longman.

Lynch-Brown, C., & Tomlinson, C. M. (1993). *Essentials of children's literature.* Boston: Allyn and Bacon.

Lynch-Brown, C., & Tomlinson, C. M. (1999). *Essentials of children's literature* (3rd ed.). Boston: Allyn and Bacon.

McClure, A. (1990). *Sunrises and songs: Reading and writing poetry in an elementary classroom.* Portsmouth, NH: Heinemann.

Meigs, C., Eaton, A. T., Nesbitt, E., & Viguers, R. H. (1969). *A critical history of children's literature* (rev. ed.). London: Macmillan.

Merryfield, M. M., & White, C. S. (1996). Issues-centered global education. In R. W. Evans & D. W. Saxe (Eds.), *Handbook on teaching social issues: NCSS Bulletin 93* (pp. 177–187). Washington, DC: National Council for the Social Studies.

Nodelman, P. (1988). *Words about pictures: The narrative art of children's picture books.* Athens, GA: University of Georgia Press.

Nodelman, P. (1996). *The pleasures of children's literature* (2nd ed.). White Plains, NY: Longman.

Oden, P. (1992). Geography is everywhere in children's literature. *Journal of Geography, 91,* 151–158.

Orlev, U. (1956/1979). *The lead soldiers.* Trans. H. Halkin. New York: Taplinger.

Orlev, U. (1998). *The sandgame.* Trans. H. Halkin. Israel: The Ghetto Fighters' House.

Pérez Díaz, E. (1996). Central and South America and the Caribbean. In P. Hunt & S. Ray (Eds.), *International companion encyclopedia of children's literature* (pp. 882–892). New York: Routledge.

Pratt, L., & Beaty, J. J. (1999). *Transcultural children's literature.* Columbus, OH: Merrill.

Rochman, H. (1993). *Against borders: Promoting books for a multicultural world.* Chicago: American Library Association.

Roger, M. D. (1978). Translation—Art, Science, or Craft. In Klingberg, G., Ørvig, M., and Amor, S. (Eds.), *Children's books in translation: The situation and the problems* (pp. 104–112). Stockholm: Almqvist & Wiksell.

Shavit, Z. (1996). Hebrew and Israeli. In P. Hunt & S. Ray (Eds.), *International companion encyclopedia of children's literature* (pp. 783–788). New York: Routledge.

Sloan, G. D. (1991). *The child as critic: Teaching literature in elementary and middle schools.* New York: Teachers College Press.

Something about the author autobiography series (vol. 21). (1996). Niki Daly (pp. 75–102). Detroit: Gale.

Stan, S. (1999). Going global: World literature for American children. *Theory into Practice, 38,* 168–177.

Stewig, J. W. (1992). Reading pictures, reading text: Some similarities. *The New Advocate, 5* (1), 11–22.

Stewig, J. W. (1995). *Looking at picture books.* Fort Atkinson, WI: Highsmith.

Stottele, C. (1997). 16th Biennale of Illustrations Bratislava, 1997. *Bookbird: World of Children's Books, 35* (4), 43–44.

Sutherland, Z. (1999). Mildred L. Batchelder, 1901–1998. *The Horn Book Magazine, 75*(1), 100–102.

Sutherland, Z., & Arbuthnot, M. H. (1991). *Children and books* (8th ed.). New York: HarperCollins.

Telgen, D. ((Ed.). (1994). *Something about the author.* Detroit: Gale.

Temple, C., Martinez, M., Yokota, J., & Naylor, A. (1998). *Children's books in children's hands: An introduction to their literature.* Boston: Allyn and Bacon.

Tomlinson, C. M. (Ed.). (1998). *Children's books from other countries.* Lanham, MD: Scarecrow.

Tunnell, G., & Ammon, J. (1993). Teaching the Holocaust through trade books. In M. O. Tunnell & R. Ammon (Eds.), *The story of ourselves: Teaching history through children's literature* (pp. 115–134). Portsmouth, NH: Heinemann.

Tway, E., & White, M. L. (1988). Literature and international understanding. In B. F. Nelms (Ed.), *Literature in the classroom: Readers, texts, and contexts.* Urbana, IL: National Council of Teachers of English.

Wah, W. Y., & Ho, L. (1996). China. In P. Hunt & S. Ray (Eds.), *International companion encyclopedia of children's literature* (pp. 830–835). New York: Routledge.

White, M. (1992). Children's books from other languages: A study of successful translations. *Journal of Youth Services in Libraries, 5,* 261–275.

Yenika-Agbaw, V. (1998). Images of West Africa in children's books: Replacing old stereotypes with new ones? *The New Advocate, 11,* 203–218.

Zack, V. (1991). "It was the worst of times": Learning about the Holocaust through literature. *Language Arts, 68,* 42–48.

CHILDREN'S BOOKS CITED

Aardema, V. (1995). *How the ostrich got its long neck.* Ill. M. Brown. New York: Scholastic.

Aardema, V. (1997). *Anansi does the impossible.* Ill. L Desimini. New York: Atheneum.

Abelove, J. (1998). *Go and come back.* New York: DK Publishing.

Ada, A. F. (1997). *Gathering the sun: An alphabet in Spanish and English.* Trans. R. Zubizarreta. Ill. S. Silva. New York: Lothrop, Lee and Shepard.

Ada, A. F. (1998). *Under the royal palms: A childhood in Cuba.* New York: Atheneum.

Agard, J., & Nichols, G. (1995). *No hickory, no dickory, no dock: Caribbean nursery rhymes.* Ill. C. Jabar. Cambridge, MA: Candlewick.

Almagor, G. (1995). *Under the domim tree.* Trans. H. Schenker. New York: Simon & Schuster.

Almond, D. (1999). *Skellig.* New York: Delacorte.

Ancona, G. (1997). *Mayeros: A Yucatec Maya family.* New York: Lothrop, Lee and Shepard.

Ancona, G. (1999). *Carnaval.* San Diego, CA: Harcourt Brace.

Anderson, L. H. (1996). *Ndito runs.* Ill. A. van der Merwe. New York: Henry Holt.

Arcellana, F. (1999). *The mats.* Ill. H. Alègrè. La Jolla, CA: Kane/Miller.

August House. (1994). *Multicultural tales to tell* (audiobook). Little Rock, AR: Author.

Baillie, A. (1992). *Little brother.* New York: Viking.

Barboza, S. (1994). *Door of no return: The legend of Gorée Island.* New York: Dutton.

Barrie, J. M. (1906). *Peter Pan in Kensington Gardens.* Ill. A. Rackham. London:Weathervane Scribner's.

Bateman, R. (1998). *Safari.* Boston: Little Brown.

Bishop, G. (1996). *Maui and the sun: A Maori tale.* New York: North-South.

Bitton-Jackson, L. (1997). *I have lived a thousand years: Growing up in the Holocaust.* New York: Simon & Schuster.

Björk, C. (1987). *Linnea in Monet's garden.* Trans. J. Sandin. Ill. L. Anderson. New York: Farrar, Straus and Giroux.

Blake, W. (1789/1966). *Songs of innocence.* Ill. E. Raskin. New York: Doubleday.

Bloom, V. (1997). *Fruits: A Caribbean counting poem.* Ill. D. Axtell. New York: Holt.

Bogacki, T. (1996). *Cat and mouse.* New York: Farrar, Straus and Giroux.

Bognomo, J. E. (1999). *Madoulina: A girl who wanted to go to school.* Honesdale, PA: Boyds Mills.

Bohlmeijer, A. (1996). *Something very sorry.* Trans. Author. Boston: Houghton Mifflin.

Bond, R. (1995). *Binya's blue umbrella.* Honesdale, PA: Boyds Mills.

Boudalika, L. (1998). *If you could be my friend.* Trans. A. Landes. New York: Orchard.

Brewster, H. (1996). *Anastasia's album: The last tsar's youngest daughter tells her own story.* New York: Hyperion.

Brusca, M. C. (1994). *My mamma's little ranch on the pampas.* New York: Holt.

Burnett, F. H. (1911/1988). *The secret garden.* Ill. T. Tudor. New York: Viking.

Burningham, J. (1971). *Mr. Gumpy's outing.* New York: Holt.

Burroughs, E. R. (1914/1999). *Tarzan of the apes.* Adapt. R. Moore. New York: Aladdin.

Campbell, E. (1998). *Papa Tembo.* San Diego, CA: Harcourt Brace.

Carling, A. L. (1998). *Mama & Papa have a store.* New York: Dial.

Carroll, L. (1865/1989). *Alice's adventures in Wonderland.* Ill. J. Tenniel. New York: Philomel.

Carroll, L. (1871/1977). *Through the looking glass.* Ill. J. Tenniel. New York: St. Martin's.

Carroll, L. (1986). *The walrus and the carpenter.* Ill. J. B. Zalben. New York: Holt.

Case, D. (1995). *92 Queens Road.* New York: Farrar, Straus and Giroux.

Cha, D. (1996). *Dia's story cloth: The Hmong people's journey to freedom.* Stitched by C. & N. T. Cha. New York: Lee & Low.

Charles, F. (Comp.). (1996). *A Caribbean counting book.* Ill. R. Arenson. Boston: Houghton Mifflin.

Cherry, L., & Plotkin, M. J. (1998). *The shaman's apprentice: A tale of the Amazon rain forest.* Ill. L. Cherry. San Diego, CA: Harcourt Brace.

Child, L. (1999). *I want a pet.* Berkeley, CA: Tricycle.

Cho, S. (1994). *The gas we pass (the story of farts).* La Jolla, CA: Kane/Miller.

Choi, S. N. (1991). *Year of impossible goodbyes.* Boston: Houghton Mifflin.

Collodi, C. (1891/1988). *The adventures of Pinocchio.* Ill. R. Innocenti. New York: Knopf.

Conlon-McKenna, M. (1990). *Under the hawthorne tree.* New York: Holiday House.

Cooper, F. (1996). *Mandela: From the life of the South African statesman.* New York: Philomel.

Cornette. (1999). *Purple coyote.* Ill. Rochette. New York: Doubleday.

Dahl, R. (1984). *Boy.* New York: Farrar, Straus and Giroux.

Dalokay, V. (1994). *Sister Shako and Kolo the goat: Memories of my childhood in Turkey.* Trans. G. Ener. New York: Lothrop, Lee and Shepard.

Daly, N. (1986). *Not so fast Songololo.* New York: Atheneum.

Daly, N. (1995). *Why the sun and moon live in the sky.* New York: Lothrop, Lee and Shepard.

Daly, N. (1998). *Bravo, Zan Angelo! A commedia dell'arte tale.* New York: Farrar, Straus and Giroux.

Daly, N. (1999). *Jamela's dress.* New York: Farrar, Straus and Giroux.

de Brunhoff, J. (1967). *The story of Babar, the little elephant.* New York: Random House.

de Jenkins, L. B. (1996). *So loud a silence.* New York: Lodestar.

de Saint-Exupèry, A. (1943). *The little prince.* Trans. K. Woods. New York: Harcourt.

Delgado, M. I. (1996). *Chave's memories=Los recuerdos de Chave.* Ill. Y. Symank. Houston, TX: Arte Público.

Demi. (1986). *Dragon kites and dragonflies: A collection of Chinese nursery rhymes.* San Diego, CA: Harcourt Brace.

Demi. (1991). *Chingis Khan.* New York: Holt.

Demi. (1997). *One grain of rice: A mathematical folktale.* New York: Scholastic.

Diakité, B. W. (1999). *The hatseller and the monkeys.* New York: Scholastic.

Dodge, M. M. (1865/1975). *Hans Brinker, or the silver skates.* Ill. H. Van Stockum. Philadelphia: Collins.

Dolphin, L. (1993). *Neve Shalom/Wahat al-Salam: Oasis of peace.* Photo. B. Dolphin. New York: Scholastic.

Dolphin, L. (1997). *Our journey from Tibet: Based on a true story.* Photo. N. J. Johnson. New York: Dutton.

Eduar, G. (1999). *Dream journey.* New York: Orchard.

Farmer, N. (1996). *A girl named Disaster.* New York: Orchard.

Filipovic, Z. (1994). *Zlata's diary: A child's life in Sarajevo.* Trans. C. Pribichevich-Zoric. New York: Viking.

Fine, A. (1994). *Flour babies.* Boston: Little, Brown.

Finger, C. (1924). *Tales from silver lands.* Ill. P. Honore. Garden City, NY: Doubleday.

Fletcher, S. (1998). *Shadow spinner.* New York: Atheneum.

Foreman, M. (1989). *War boy: A country childhood.* New York: Arcade.

Foreman, M. (1995). *After the war was over.* New York: Arcade.

Fox, M. (1989). *Koala Lou.* Ill. P. Lofts. San Diego, CA: Harcourt Brace.

Fox, M. (1990). *Possum magic.* Ill. J. Vivas. San Diego, CA: Harcourt Brace.

Fox, M. (1996). *Wombat divine.* Ill. K. Argent. San Diego, CA: Harcourt Brace.

Frank, R. (1986). *No hero for the kaiser.* Trans. P. Crampton. New York: Lothrop, Lee and Shepard.

Franklin, K. L., & McGirr, N. (1996). *Out of the dump: Writings and photographs by children from Guatemala.* Trans. K. L. Franklin. New York: Lothrop, Lee and Shepard.

Freedman, R. (1997). *Out of darkness: The story of Louis Braille.* Ill. K. Kiesler. New York: Clarion.

Freeman, D. (1968). *Corduroy.* New York: Viking.

Gallaz, C., & Innocenti, R. (1985). *Rose Blanche.* Trans. M. Coventry & R. Graglia. Ill. R. Innocenti. Mankato, MN: Creative Editions.

Garay, L. (1997). *Pedrito's day.* New York: Orchard.

Gollub, M. (1998). *Cool melons—turn to frogs!: The life and poems of Issa.* Ill. K. G. Stone. New York: Lee & Low.

Gomi, T. (1993). *Everyone poops.* Trans. A. M. Stinchecum. La Jolla, CA: Kane/Miller.

González, L. M. (1997). *Señor Cat's romance and other favorite stories from Latin America.* Ill. L. Delacre. New York: Scholastic.

Goodsmith, L. (1993). *The children of Mauritania: Days in the desert and by the river shore.* Minneapolis, MN: Carolrhoda.

Gorbachev, V. (1998). *Nicky and the big,bad wolves.* New York: North-South.

Gordon, S. (1987). *Waiting for the rain: A novel of South Africa.* New York: Orchard.

Grahame, K. (1908/1961). *The wind in the willows.* New York: Scribner's.

Grant, N. (1997). *Eric the Red: The Viking adventurer.* Ill. V. Ambrus. New York: Oxford University Press.

Green, R. (1996). *Tutankhamum.* Danbury, CT: Watts.

Gunning, M. (1993). *Not a copper penny in me house: Poems from the Caribbean.* Ill. F. Lessac. Honesdale, PA: Wordsong/Boyds Mills.

Gunning, M. (1998). *Under the breadfruit tree: Island poems.* Ill. F. Vanden Broeck. Honesdale, PA: Boyds Mills.

Hamanaka, S. (1995). *On the wings of peace.* New York: Clarion.

Hanson, R. (1995). *The tangerine tree.* Ill. H. Stevenson. New York: Clarion.

Heide, F., & Gilliland, J. H. (1990). *The day of Ahmed's secret.* New York: Lothrop, Lee and Shepard.

Heide, F. P., & Gilliland, J. H. (1999). *The house of wisdom.* Ill. M. Grandpré. New York: DK Publishers.

Hickox, R. (1998). *The golden sandal: A Middle Eastern Cinderella story.* Ill. W. Hillenbrand. New York: Holiday House.

Hidaka, M. (1986). *Girl from the snow country.* Trans. A. M. Stinchecum. Brooklyn, NY: Kane/Miller.

Ho, M. (1996a). *Hush: A Thai lullaby.* Ill. H. Meade. New York: Orchard.

Ho, M. (1996b). *Maples in the mist: Children's poems from the Tang Dynasty.* Ill. J. Tseng & M. Tseng. New York: Lothrop, Lee and Shepard.

Ho, M., & Ros, S. (1995). *The two brothers*. Ill. J. Tseng & M. Tseng. New York: Lothrop, Lee and Shepard.

Hoestlandt, J. (1995). *Star of fear, star of hope*. Trans. M. Polizzotti. Ill. J. Kang. New York: Walker.

Hoffman, M. (1991). *Amazing Grace*. Ill. C. Binch. New York: Dial.

Hoffman, M. (1995). *Grace & family*. Ill. C. Binch. London: Frances Lincoln.

Hollyer, B. (1999). *Wake up, world! A day in the life of children around the world*. New York: Holt.

Holtwijk, I. (1999). *Asphalt angels*. Trans. W. Boeke. Asheville, NC: Front Street.

Holub, J. (1997). *The robber and me*. Trans. E. D. Crawford. New York: Holt.

Holzwarth, W. (1999). *I'm José and I'm okay (three stories from Bolivia)*. Trans. L. McKenna. Ill. Yatiyawi Studios. New York: Kane/Miller.

Hoobler, D., & Hoobler, T. (1999). *The ghost in the Tokaido inn*. New York: Philomel.

Horenstein, H. (1997). *Baseball in the barrios*. San Diego, CA: Harcourt Brace.

Hoshino, M. (1994). *The grizzly bear family book*. Trans. K. Calligan-Taylor. New York: North-South.

Houston, G. (1992). *My great-aunt Arizona*. Ill. S. C. Lamb. New York: HarperCollins.

Hughes, M. (1993). *A handful of seeds*. Ill. L. Garay. New York: Orchard.

Hürlimann, R. (1974). *The cat and mouse who shared a house*. Trans. A. Bell. New York: Walck.

Jacobs, J. (1890/1967). *English fairy tales*. Ill. J. D. Batten. New York: Dover.

Jacobs, J. (1892/1971). *Celtic fairy tales*. New York: World.

James, J. A. (1999). *The drums of Noto Hanto*. Ill. Tsukushi. New York: DK Publishing.

Jeunesse, G., & de Bourgoing, P. (1992). *The egg*. Trans. K. Backstein. Ill. R. Mettler. New York: Scholastic.

Jiang, J. (1997). *Red scarf girl: A memoir of the Cultural Revolution*. New York: HarperCollins.

Johnston, J. (1998). *The only outcast*. Toronto: Tundra.

Johnston, T. (1996). *My Mexico/México mío*. Ill. F. J. Sierra. New York: Putnam.

Johnston, T. (1997). *Day of the dead*. Ill. J. Winter. San Diego, CA: Harcourt Brace.

Jordan, M., & Jordan, T. (1995). *Angel Falls: A South American journey*. New York: Kingfisher.

Joseph, L. (1990). *Coconut kind of day: Island poems*. Ill. S. Speidel. New York: Lothrop, Lee and Shepard.

Joseph, L. (1998). *Jump up time: A Trinidad carnival story*. Ill. L. Saport. New York: Clarion.

Keister, D. (1995). *Fernando's Gift—El regalo de Fernando*. San Francisco: Sierra Club.

Keselman, G. (1999). *The gift*. Trans. L. McKenna. Ill. P. Montserrat. New York: Kane/Miller.

Kessler, C. (1995a). *All the king's animals: The return of endangered wildlife to Swaziland*. Honesdale, PA: Boyds Mills.

Kessler, C. (1995b). *One night: A story from the desert*. Ill. I. Schoenherr. New York: Philomel.

Khan, R. (1998). *The roses in my carpets*. Ill. R. Himler. New York: Holiday House.

Kharms, D. (1996). *First second*. Trans. R. Peaver. Ill. M. Rosenthal. New York: Farrar, Straus and Giroux.

Kherdian, D. (1997). *The rose's smile: Farizad of the Arabian nights*. Ill. S. Vitale. New York: Holt.

Kim, H. (1996). *The long season of rain*. New York: Holt.

Kindersley, B., & Kindersley, A. (1995). *Children just like me*. New York: DK Publishing.

Kipling, R. (1902/1996). *Just so stories*. Ill. B. Moser. New York: Morrow.

Klinting, L. (1996a). *Bruno the carpenter*. New York: Henry Holt.

Klinting, L. (1996b). *Bruno the tailor*. New York: Henry Holt.

Kodama, T. (1995). *Shin's tricycle*. Trans. K. Hokumen-Jones. Ill. N. Ando. New York: Walker.

Kurtz, J. (1994). *Fire on the mountain*. Ill. E. B. Lewis. New York: Simon and Schuster.

Kurtz, J. (1997). *Trouble*. Ill. D. Bernhard. San Diego, CA: Gulliver/Harcourt Brace.

Kurtz, J. (1998). *The storyteller's beads*. San Diego, CA: Harcourt Brace.

Lachner, D. (1996). *Look out, Cinder!* Trans. R. Lanning. Ill. E. Sopko. New York: North-South.

Laird, E. (1991). *Kiss the dust*. London: Mammoth.

Lang, A. (1889/1965). *The blue fairy book*. Ill. H. J. Ford & G. D. Jacomb Hood. New York: Dover.

Lang, A. (1910/1968). *The lilac fairy book*. Ill. H. J. Ford. New York: Dover.

Langley, A. (1998). *Hans Christian Andersen*. Ill. T. Morris. New York: Oxford University Press.

Lankford, M. D. (1998). *Dominoes around the world*. Ill. K. Dugan. New York: Morrow.

Lasky, K. (1992). *Surtsey: The newest place on earth*. Photos. C. G. Knight. New York: Hyperion.

Lasky, K. (1998). *Shadows in the dawn: The lemurs of Madagascar*. Photos. C. G. Knight. San Diego, CA: Harcourt Brace.

Leapman, M. (1998). *Witnesses to war: Eight true-life stories of Nazi persecution*. New York: Viking.

Lear, E. (1846/1976). *The book of nonsense*. New York: Garland.

Leder, J. M. (1996). *A Russian Jewish family*. Minneapolis, MN: Lerner.

Leigh, N. K. (1993). *Learning to swim in Swaziland*. New York: Scholastic.

Les Chats Pelés. (1996). *Long live music!* Trans. C. Volk. San Diego, CA: Harcourt Brace.

Lessac, F. (1987/1994). *Caribbean canvas*. Honesdale, PA: Boyds Mills.

Levine, E. (1995). *Anna Pavlova: Genius of the dance*. New York: Scholastic.

Lewin, H. (1983). *Jafta—The journey*. Minneapolis, MN: Carolrhoda.

Lewin, T. (1995). *Sacred river*. New York: Clarion.

Lewin, T. (1998). *The storytellers*. New York: Lothrop, Lee and Shepard.

Lewis, J. P. (1994). *The frog princess*. Ill. G. Spirin. New York: Dial.

Lindgren, A. (1954). *Pippi Longstocking*. Trans. F. Lamborn. London: Puffin.

Lindgren, A. (1983). *Ronia the robber's daughter*. Trans. P. Crampton. New York: Penguin.

Little, J. (1986). *Hey world, here I am!* Ill. S. Truesdell. New York: Harper.

Little, J. (1997). *The belonging place*. New York: Viking.

Lobel, A. (1998). *No pretty pictures: A child of war*. New York: Greenwillow.

London, J. (1996). *The village basket weaver*. Ill. G. Crespo. New York: Dutton.

Macaulay, D. (1988). *The way things work*. New York: DK Publishing.

Mado, M. (1992). *The animals*. Trans. The Empress Michiko of Japan. Ill. M. Anno. New York: McElderry.

Mado, M. (1998). *The magic pocket*. Trans. The Empress Michiko of Japan. Ill. M. Anno. New York: McElderry.

Malam, J. (1998). *Vincent Van Gogh*. Minneapolis, MN: Carolrhoda.

Malone, M. (1996). *A Guatemalan family*. Minneapolis, MN: Lerner.

Margolies, B. (1994). *Olbalbal: A day in Maasailand*. New York: Macmillan.

Marsden, J. (1998). *Checkers*. Boston: Houghton Mifflin.

Maruki, T. (1982). *Hiroshima no pika*. Trans. Kurita-Bando Literary Agency. New York: Lothrop, Lee and Shepard.

McKay, L., Jr. (1995). *Caravan*. Ill. D. Ligasan. New York: Lee & Low.

McKissack, P., & McKissack, F. (1994). *The royal kingdoms of Ghana, Mali, and Songhay: Life in Medieval Africa*. New York: Holt.

Menick, S. (1998). *The muffin child*. New York: Philomel.

Mennel, W. (1996). *Henry & Horace clean up*. Trans. M. Martens. Ill. G. Dürr. New York: North-South.

Milne, A. A. (1924). *When we were very young*. Ill. E. H. Shepard. New York: Dutton.

Milne, A. A. (1926). *Winnie the pooh*. Ill. E. H. Shepard. New York: Dutton.

Milne, A. A. (1927). *Now we are six*. Ill. E. H. Shepard. New York: Dutton.

Min, W. (1999). *Peter's patchwork dream*. New York: Barefoot.

Mitchell, P. (1997). *Gandhi: The father of modern India*. Ill. M. Mitra. New York: Oxford University Press.

Mochizuki, K. (1997). *Passage to freedom: The Sugihara story*. Ill. D. Lee. New York: Lee & Low.

Mollel, T. M. (1988). *Rhino's boy*. New Zealand: Outriggers.

Mollel, T. M. (1991). *Orphan boy*. Ill. P. Morin. New York: Clarion.

Mollel, T. M. (1993). *The princess who lost her hair: An Akamba legend*. Ill. C. Reasoner. Mahwah, NJ: Troll.

Mollel, T. M. (1994). *The flying tortoise: An Igbo tale*. Ill. B. Spurll. New York: Clarion.

Mollel, T. M. (1995). *Big boy*. Ill. E. B. Lewis. New York: Clarion.

Mollel, T. M. (1996). *Ananse's feast: An Ashanti tale*. Ill. A. Glass. New York: Clarion.

Mollel, T. M. (1997). *Kele's secret*. Ill. C. Stock. New York: Lodestar.

Mollel, T. M. (1999). *My rows and piles of coins*. Ill. E. B. Lewis. New York: Clarion.

Mollel, T. M. (2000). *Subira Subira*. Ill. L. Saport. New York: Clarion.

Montgomery, L. M. (1908/1983). *Anne of Green Gables*. New York: Putnam.

Moodie, F. (1996). *Nabulela*. New York: Farrar, Straus and Giroux.

Mori, K. (1993). *Shizuko's daughter*. New York: Holt.

Morin, P. (1998). *Animal dreaming: An Aboriginal dreamtime story*. San Diego, CA: Harcourt Brace.

Musgrove, M. (1976). *Ashanti to Zulu: African traditions*. Ill. L. Dillon & D. Dillon. New York: Dial.

Naidoo, B. (1988). *Journey to Jo'burg: A South African story*. New York: Harper.

Naidoo, B. (1997). *No turning back: A novel of South Africa*. New York: HarperCollins.

Napoli, D. J. (1997). *Stones in water*. New York: Dutton.

Nesbit, E. (1987). *Long ago when I was young*. Ill. G. Buchanan & E. Ardizzone. New York: Dial.

Nhuong, H. Q. (1997). *Water buffalo days: Growing up in Vietnam*. Ill. J. Tseng & M. Tseng. New York: HarperCollins.

Nichols, G. (1997). *Asana and the animals: A book of pet poems*. Ill. S. Adams. Cambridge, MA: Candlewick.

Njeng, P. Y. (1999). *Vacation in the village: A story from West Africa*. Honesdale, PA: Boyds Mills.

Nöstlinger, C. (1977). *Konrad*. Trans. A. Bell. Danbury, CT: Watts.

Nye, N. S. (1997). *Habibi*. New York: Simon & Schuster.

Nye, N. S. (Sel.). (1995). *The tree is older than you are: A bilingual gathering of poems & stories from Mexico with paintings by Mexican artists*. New York: Simon & Schuster.

Nye, N. S. (Sel.). (1998). *The space between our footsteps: Poems and paintings from the Middle East*. New York: Simon & Schuster.

Olaleye, I. (1995). *The distant talking drum: Poems from Nigeria*. Ill. F. Lessac. Honesdale, PA: Boyds Mills.

Olaleye, I. (1998). *Lake of the big snake: An African rain forest adventure*. Ill. C. Shepard. Honesdale, PA: Boyds Mills.

Onyefulu, I. (1993). *A is for Africa*. New York: Cobblehill.

Onyefulu, I. (1995). *Emeka's gift: An African counting story*. New York: Cobblehill.

Onyefulu, I. (1996). *Ogbo: Sharing life in an African village*. San Diego, CA: Harcourt.

Orlev, U. (1984). *The island on Bird Street*. Trans. H. Halkin. Boston: Houghton Mifflin.

Orlev, U. (1991). *The man from the other side*. Trans. H. Halkin. Boston: Houghton Mifflin.

Orlev, U. (1993). *Lydia, queen of Palestine*. Trans. H. Halkin. Boston: Houghton Mifflin.

Orlev, U. (1995). *The lady with the hat*. Trans. H. Halkin. Boston: Houghton Mifflin.

Ousseimi, M. (1995). *Caught in the crossfire: Growing up in a war zone*. New York: Walker.

Park, F., & Park, G. (1998). *My freedom trip*. Honesdale, PA: Boyds Mills.

Park, R. (1984). *Playing Beatie Bow*. New York: Atheneum.

Pausewang, G. (1996). *The final journey*. Trans. P. Crampton. New York: Viking.

Perols, S. (1997). *Endangered animals*. New York: Scholastic.

Perrault, C. (1697). *Tales of times past*. (Reprinted 1993 as *The complete fairy tales of Charles Perrault*. Trans. N. Philip & N. Somborowski. Ill. S. Holmes. New York: Clarion.)

Pfister, M. (1992). *The rainbow fish*. Trans. J. A. James. New York: North-South.

Pfister, M. (1997). *Milo and the magical stones*. Trans. M. Martens. New York: North-South.

Philip, N. (Ed.). (1998). *War and the pity of war*. Ill. M. McCurdy. New York: Clarion.

Pitkänen, M. A. (1990). *The children of Nepal*. Minneapolis, MN: Carolrhoda.

Pohl, P., & Gieth, K. (1999). *I miss you, I miss you!* Trans. R. Greenwald. New York: R & S Books.

Popov, N. (1996). *Why?* New York: North-South.

Pressler, M. (1998). *Halinka*. Trans. E. D. Crawford. New York: Holt.

Rabinovici, S. (1998). *Thanks to my mother*. Trans. J. Skofield. New York: Dial.

Rahaman, V. (1996). *O Christmas tree*. Ill. F. Lessac. Honesdale, PA: Boyds Mills.

Rahaman, V. (1997). *A little salmon for witness: A story from Trinidad*. Ill. S. Speidel. New York: Dutton.

Reider, K. (1997). *Snail started it!* Trans. R. Lanning. Ill. A. von Roehl. New York: North-South.

Reiss, J. (1972). *The upstairs room*. New York: Crowell.

Reuter, B. B. (1989). *Buster's world*. Trans. A. Bell. New York: Dutton.

Reuter, B. B. (1994). *The boys from St. Petri*. Trans. A. Bell. New York: Dutton.

Reynolds, J. (1991). *Sahara: Vanishing cultures*. San Diego, CA: Harcourt Brace

Reynolds, J. (1992). *Down under: Vanishing cultures*. San Diego, CA: Harcourt Brace.

Richter, H. P. (1970/1987). *Friedrich*. Trans. E. Kroll. New York: Penguin.

Romanelli, S. (1995). *Little Bobo*. Ill. H. de Beer. New York: North-South.

Romanelli, S. (1997). *Little Bobo saves the day*. Ill. H. de Beer. New York: North-South.

Rondón, J. (1994). *The absent-minded toad*. Trans. K. Corbett. Ill. M. Cabrera. Brooklyn, NY: Kane/Miller.

Rosen, M. (1999). *Rover*. Ill. N. Layton. New York: Doubleday.

Rowling, J. K. (1998). *Harry Potter and the sorcerer's stone*. New York: Scholastic.

Russell, C. Y. (1999). *Child bride*. Honesdale, PA: Boyds Mills.

Salisbury, G. (1994). *Under the blood-red sun*. New York: Delacorte.

Sancha, S. (1989). *Walter Dragun's town: Crafts and trades in the Middle Ages* . New York: Crowell.

San Souci, R. (1998). *Cendrillon: A Caribbean Cinderella*. Ill. B. Pinkney. New York: Simon & Schuster.

Schami, R. (1990). *A hand full of stars*. Trans. R. Lesser. New York: Dutton.

Schneider, A. (1998). *Good-bye, Vivi!* Trans. J. A. James. Ill. M. Dusíková. New York: North-South.

Schwartz, D. M. (1995). *Yanomami: People of the Amazon*. Photo. V. Englebert. New York: Lothrop, Lee and Shepard.

Shea, P. D. (1995). *The whispering cloth: A refugee's story*. Ill. A. Riggio. Stitched by Y. Yang. Honesdale, PA: Boyds Mills.

Shephard, A. (1998). *The crystal heart: A Vietnamese legend*. Ill. J. D. Fiedler. New York: Atheneum.

Siegel, A. (1981). *Upon the head of the goat: A childhood in Hungary, 1939–1944*. New York: Farrar, Straus and Giroux.

Silverman, R. L. (1997). *A Bosnian family*. Photo. S. Silverman. Minneapolis, MN: Lerner.

Sís, P. (1998). *Tibet through the red box*. New York: Farrar, Straus and Giroux.

Sisulu, E. B. (1996). *The day Gogo went to vote: South Africa April 1994*. Ill. S. Wilson. Boston: Little, Brown.

Slobodkina, E. (1947). *Caps for sale*. New York: W. R. Scott.

Smith, R., & Schmidt, M. J. (1998). *In the forest with the elephants*. San Diego, CA: Harcourt Brace.

Smucker, B. (1998). *Selina and the shoo-fly pie*. Ill. J. Wilson. Quilts, L. A. Holliday. Toronto: Stoddart Kids.

Solá, M. (1997). *Angela weaves a dream: The story of a young Maya artist*. Photo. J. J. Foxx. New York: Hyperion.

Sortland, B. (1999). *Anna's art adventure*. Trans. J. Anderson. Ill. L. Elling. Minneapolis, MN: Carolrhoda.

Spier, P. (1980). *People*. Garden City, NY: Doubleday.

Spivak, D. (1997). *Grass sandals: The travels of Basho.* Ill. Demi. New York: Atheneum.

Spyri, J. (1880, reprint 1945). *Heidi.* Trans. H. B. Dole. Ill. W. Sharp. New York: Grosset & Dunlap.

Stanley, D., & Vennema, P. (1994). *Cleopatra.* Ill. D. Stanley. New York: Morrow.

Staples, S. F. (1989). *Shabanu, daughter of the wind.* New York: Knopf.

Stevenson, R. L. (1883/1981). *Treasure island.* Ill. N. C. Wyeth. New York: Scribner's.

Stevenson, R. L. (1885/1985). *A child's garden of verses.* Ill. M. Foreman. New York: Delacorte.

Stewart, D. (1996). *Gift of the sun: A tale from South Africa.* Ill. J. Daly. New York: Farrar, Straus and Giroux.

Stuve-Bodeen, S. (1998). *Elizabeti's doll.* Ill. C. Hale. New York: Lee & Low.

Sutcliffe, R. (1990). *The shining company.* New York: Farrar, Straus and Giroux.

Te Kanawa, K. (1989). *Land of the long white cloud: Maori myths, tales and legends.* Ill. M. Foreman. New York: Arcade.

Temple, F. (1995). *Tonight, by sea.* New York: Orchard.

Tolstoy, A. (1999). *The gigantic turnip.* Ill. N. Sharkey. Brooklyn, NY: Barefoot Books.

Torres, L. (1995). *Saturday sancocho/El sancocho del sábado.* New York: Farrar, Straus and Giroux.

Trottier, M. (1998). *The walking stick.* Ill. A. G. Galouchko. Toronto: Stoddart Kids.

Tsubakiyama, M. H. (1999). *Mei-Mei loves the morning.* Ill. C. Van Wright & Y-H. Hu. Morton Grove, IL: Albert Whitman.

Twain, M. (1888/1989). *The adventures of Tom Sawyer.* New York: Penguin.

Valat, P. (1998). *Sports.* New York: Scholastic.

van der Rol, R., & Verhoeven, R. (1993). *Anne Frank, beyond the diary: A photographic remembrance.* Trans. T. Langham & P. Peters. New York: Viking.

Van Laan, N. (1991). *The legend of El Dorado.* Ill. B. Vidal. New York: Knopf.

Van Laan, N. (1998a). *So say the little monkeys.* Ill. Y. Heo. New York: Atheneum.

Van Laan, N. (1998b). *The magic bean tree: A legend from Argentina.* Ill. B. Vidal. Boston: Houghton Mifflin.

van Loon, H. W. (1921). *The story of mankind.* New York: Boni & Liveright.

Vendrell, C. S. (1999). *Jon's moon.* New York: Kane/Miller.

Verne, J. (1869/1995). *Twenty thousand leagues under the sea.* New York: Puffin.

Vojtech, A., & Sturges, P. (1996). *Marushka and the month brothers.* Ill. A. Vojtech. New York: North-South.

Volavková, H. (Ed.). (1993). *. . . I never saw another butterfly . . .* New York: Schocken.

Vos, I. (1991). *Hide and seek.* Trans. T. Edelstein & I. Smidt. Boston: Houghton Mifflin.

Wassiljewa, T. (1997). *Hostage to war: A true story.* Trans. A. Trenter. New York: Scholastic.

Watkins, Y. K. (1986). *So far from the bamboo grove.* New York: Lothrop, Lee and Shepard.

Weninger, B. (1996). *Ragged bear.* Trans. M. Martens. Ill. A. Marks. New York: North-South.

Wheatley, N., & Rawlins, D. (1987). *My place.* Long Beach, CA: Australia in Print.

Wild, M., & Vivas, J. (1991). *Let the celebrations begin!* New York: Orchard.

Williams, K. L. (1998). *Painted dreams.* Ill. C. Stock. New York: Lothrop, Lee and Shepard.

Williams, L. E. (1995). *The long silk strand: A grandmother's legacy to her granddaughter.* Ill. G. Bochak. Honesdale, PA: Boyds Mills.

Williams, M. (1922/1991). *The velveteen rabbit.* Ill. W. Nicholson. New York: Doubleday.

Winter, J. (1991). *Diego.* Ill. J. Winter. New York: Knopf.

Wisniewski, D. (1992). *Sundiata, lion king of Mali.* New York: Clarion.

Wisniewski, D. (1996). *Golem.* New York: Clarion.

Wolkstein, D. (1978/1997). *Bouki dances the Kokioko: A comical tale from Haiti.* Ill. J. Sweetwater. San Diego, CA: Harcourt Brace.

Wynne-Jones, T. (1995). *Some of the kinder planets.* New York: Orchard.

Wynne-Jones, T. (1998). *Stephen Fair.* New York: DK Publishing.

Wyss, J. D. (1812/1949). *The Swiss family Robinson.* Ill. L. Ward. New York: Grosset.

Yep, L. (1989/1993). *The rainbow people.* Recorded Books (audiobook).

Yep, L. (1997). *The khan's daughter: A Mongolian folktale.* Ill. J. Tseng & M. Tseng. New York: Scholastic.

Yolen, J. (Ed.). (1992). *Street rhymes around the world.* Honesdale, PA: Wordsong/Boyds Mills.

Yumoto, K. (1996). *The friends.* Trans. C. Hirano. New York: Farrar, Straus and Giroux.

Zagwÿn, D. T. (1999). *Apple batter.* Berkeley, CA: Tricycle.

Zemser, A. B. (1998). *Beyond the mango tree.* New York: Greenwillow.

Hans Christian Andersen Award Recipients

Author

2000	Ana Maria Machado–Brazil
1998	Katherine Paterson–USA
1996	Uri Orlev–Israel
1994	Michio Mado–Japan
1992	Virginia Hamilton–USA
1990	Tormod Haugen–Norway
1988	Annie M. G. Schmidt–Netherlands
1986	Patricia Wrightson–Australia
1984	Christine Nöstlinger–Austria
1982	Lygia Bojunga Nunes–Brazil
1980	Bohumil Ríha–Czechoslovakia
1978	Paula Fox–USA
1976	Cecil Bodker–Denmark
1974	Maria Gripe–Sweden
1972	Scott O'Dell–USA
1970	Gianni Rodari–Italy
1968	James Krüss–Germany
	José Maria Sanchez-Silva–Spain
1966	Tove Jansson–Finland
1964	René Guillot–France
1962	Meindert Dejong–USA
1960	Erich Kästner–Germany
1958	Astrid Lindgren–Sweden
1956	Eleanor Farjeon–Great Britain

Illustrator

2000	Anthony Browne–United Kingdom
1998	Tomi Ungerer–France
1996	Klaus Ensikat–Germany
1994	Jörg Müller–Switzerland
1992	Kveta Pacovska–Czechoslovakia
1990	Lisbeth Zwerger–Austria
1988	Dusan Kallay–Czechoslovakia
1986	Robert Ingpen–Australia
1984	Mitsumasa Anno–Japan
1982	Zbigniew Rychlicki–Poland
1980	Suekichi Akaba–Japan
1978	Svend Otto S.–Denmark
1976	Tatjana Mawrina–USSR
1974	Farshid Mesghali–Iran
1972	Ib Spang Ohlsson–Denmark
1970	Maurice Sendak–USA
1968	Jiri Trnka–Czechoslovakia
1966	Alois Carigiet–Switzerland

APPENDIX B

Mildred L. Batchelder Award Recipients

2000 *The Baboon King*, Anton Quintana, translated from Dutch by John Nieuwenhuizen (Walker)

1999 *Thanks to My Mother*, Schoschana Rabinovici, translated from German by James Skofield (Dial)

1998 *The Robber and Me*, Joseph Holub, translated from German by Elizabeth D. Crawford (Holt)

1997 *The Friends*, Kazumi Yumoto, translated from Japanese by Cathy Hirano (Farrar)

1996 *The Lady with the Hat*, Uri Orlev, translated from Hebrew by Hillel Halkin (Houghton Mifflin)

1995 *The Boys from St Petri*, Bjarne Reuter, translated from Danish by Anthea Bell (Dutton)

1994 *The Apprentice*, Pilar Molina Llorente, translated from Spanish by Robin Longshaw (Farrar)

1993 No Award

1992 *The Man from the Other Side*, Uri Orlev, translated from Hebrew by Hillel Halkin (Houghton Mifflin)

1991 *A Hand Full of Stars*, Rafik Schami, translated from German by Rika Lesser (Dutton)

1990 *Buster's World*, Bjarne Reuter, translated from Danish by Anthea Bell (Dutton)

1989 *Crutches*, Peter Härtling, translated from German by Elizabeth D. Crawford (Lothrop)

1988 *If You Didn't Have Me*, Ulf Nilsson, translated from Swedish by George Blecher and Lone Thygesen-Blecher (Macmillan)

1987 *No Hero for the Kaiser*, Rudolph Frank, translated from German by Patricia Crampton (Lothrop)

1986 *Rose Blanche*, Christopher Gallaz and Roberto Innocenti, translated from French by Martha Coventry and Richard Graglia (Creative Education)

1985 *The Island on Bird Street*, Uri Orlev, translated from Hebrew by Hillel Halkin (Houghton Mifflin)

1984 *Ronia, the Robber's Daughter*, Astrid Lindgren, translated from Swedish by Patricia Crampton (Viking)

1983 *Hiroshima No Pika*, Toshi Maruki, translated from Japanese through the Kurita-Bando Literary Agency (Lothrop)

1982 *The Battle Horse*, Harry Kullman, translated from Swedish by George Blecher and Lone Thygesen-Blecher (Bradbury)

1981 *The Winter When Time Was Frozen*, Els Pelgrom, translated from Dutch by Maryka Rudnik and Raphael Rudnik (Morrow)

1980   *The Sound of the Dragon's Feet,* Aliki Zei, translated from Greek by Edward Fenton (Dutton)

1979   *Konrad,* Christine Nöstlinger, translated from German by Anthea Bell (Watts); *Rabbit Island,* Jörg Steiner, translated from German by Ann Conrad Lammers (Harcourt)

1978   No Award

1977   *The Leopard,* Cecil Bodker, translated from Danish by Gunnar Poulsen (Atheneum)

1976   *The Cat and Mouse Who Shared a House,* Ruth Hürlimann, translated from German by Anthea Bell (Walck)

1975   *An Old Tale Carved Out of Stone,* A. Linevski, translated from Russian by Maria Polushkin (Crown)

1974   *Petros' War,* Aliki Zei, translated from Greek by Edward Fenton (Dutton)

1973   *Pulga,* S. R. Van Iterson, translated from Dutch by Alexander Gode and Alison Gode (Morrow)

1972   *Friedrich,* Hans Peter Richter, translated from German by Edite Kroll (Holt)

1971   *In the Land of Ur: The Discovery of Ancient Mesopotamia,* Hans Baumann, translated from German by Stella Humphries (Pantheon)

1970   *Wildcat Under Glass,* Aliki Zei, translated from Greek by Edward Fenton (Holt)

1969   *Don't Take Teddy,* Babbis Friis-Baastad, translated from Norwegian by Lise Somme McKinnon (Scribner's)

1968   *The Little Man,* Eric Kästner, translated from German by James Kirkup (Knopf)

APPENDIX C

Publishers of International Books

Africa World Press, Inc.
11-D Princess Rd.
Lawrenceville, NJ 08648

Annick Press
15 Patricia Avenue
Willowdale, Ontario
Canada M2M 1H9

Arte Público Press
University of Houston
4800 Calhoun
Houston, TX 77204–2090

Boyds Mills Press
815 Church St.
Honesdale, PA 18431

Candlewick Press
2067 Massachusetts Ave.
Cambridge, MA 02140

Children's Book Press
6400 Hollis St.
Everyville, CA 94604

Clarion Books
215 Park Avenue South
New York, NY 10003

DK Publishing, Inc.
95 Madison Avenue
New York, NY 10016

Farrar, Straus and Giroux
19 Union Square West
New York, NY 10003

Firefly
250 Sparks Avenue
Willowdale, Ontario
Canada M2H254

Harcourt Brace
    Children's Books
525 B. Street, Suite 1900
San Diego, CA 92101

Henry Holt and Company
115 West 18th St.
New York, NY 10011

Kane/Miller
    Book Publishers
P.O. Box 8515
La Jolla, CA 92038–8515

Kids Can Press
    (Canadian)
General Distribution Services
85 River Rock Dr., Suite 202
Buffalo, NY 14207

Lee & Low Books
95 Madison Avenue
New York, NY 10016

North-South Books
1133 Broadway, Suite 1016
New York, NY 10010

Orca Book Publishers
    (Canadian)
P.O. Box 468
Custer, WA 98240

Orchard Books
95 Madison Avenue
New York, NY 10016

Oxford University Press
98 Madison Avenue
New York, NY 10016

Peguis Publishing
100-318 McDermot Ave.
Winnipeg, Man., Canada
    R3A 0A2

Publishers Group West
Box 8843
Emeryville, California 94662
  • Groundwood Books
    (Canada)
  • Children's Book Press
  • Front Street Books
  • Roberts Rinehart
    Publishers

Stoddard Kids
    (Canadian)
General Distribution Services
85 River Rock Dr.
Suite 202
Buffalo, New York 14207

Tundra/McClelland
    & Stewart (Canadian)
P.O. Box 1030
Plattsburgh, NY 12901

APPENDIX D

Professional Resources for International Children's Literature

Bookbird: A Journal of International Children's Literature. International Board on Books for Young People. (published quarterly)

Hunt, P., & Ray, S. (Eds.). (1996). *International companion encyclopedia of children's literature.* New York: Routledge.

IBBY honour list. Basel, Switzerland: International Board on Books for Young People. (published biennially)

Jobe, R. (1993). *Cultural connections: Using literature to explore world cultures with children.* Markham, Ontario, Canada: Pembroke.

Khorana, M. (1993). *The Indian subcontinent in literature for children and young adults.* New York: Greenwood Press.

Miller-Lachman, L. (1992). *Our family, our friends, our world: An annotated guide to significant multicultural books for children and teenagers.* New Providence, NJ: R. R. Bowker.

Oso, O. (1995). *African children's and youth literature.* New York: Twayne.

Pratt, L., & Beaty, J. J. (1999). *Transcultural children's literature.* Columbus, OH: Merrill.

Rochman, H. (1993). *Against borders: Promoting books for a multicultural world.* Chicago: American Library Association.

Tomlinson, C. M. (Ed.). (1998). *Children's books from other countries.* Lanham, MD: Scarecrow.

INDEX OF SUBJECTS

NAME INDEX OF AUTHORS AND CHILDREN'S BOOKS